Praise for *Holy Ambiti*  W9-DBL-735

Chip Ingram uses Nehemiah, arguably one of the best studies on management, to show that a caring spirit and humble disposition are precursors to being the best one can be, not only as a manager, but also in any role involving one's faith, family, or vocation.

**E. Floyd Kvamme**
*Partner*
Kleiner Perkins Caufield & Byers

Chip Ingram is destined to become one of America's best Bible teachers of the 21st century. His teaching is clear with humor, depth of understanding, and practical cultural examples that capture our attention. Mercy Ships was privileged to have Chip speak to our International Board of Directors. Chip's teaching was a home run with the bases loaded, and the book of Nehemiah was readily applicable to each of our situations.

**Don Stephens**
*Founder and President*
Mercy Ships International

This book takes you to new territory. Be prepared to release your mind from old myths and embrace what God wants to do through you, right now! Be prepared to be delighted—and transformed—with Chip Ingram's insights into how God really wants to work in this present day, with regular, ordinary people. This is a book full of new possibilities and the power to change our culture.

**Walt Wilson**
*President*
Palo Alto Research Group

Did you ever wonder where in the Bible you could find an entrepreneur for God? What were his characteristics that led to success? Chip, thanks for the answers! . . . and the challenge!

**Gary Daichendt**
*Former Executive Vice President*
Cisco Systems, Inc.

# HOLY
# AMBITION

turning God-shaped dreams into reality

## chip ingram

**MOODY PUBLISHING**
CHICAGO

All Scripture quotations, unless otherwise indicated, are taken from the *Holy Bible, New International Version*®. NIV®. Copyright © 1973, 1978, 1984 by International Bible Society. Used by permission of Zondervan. All rights reserved.

Scripture quotations marked NASB are taken from the *New American Standard Bible*®, Copyright © 1960, 1962, 1963, 1968, 1971, 1972, 1973, 1975, 1977, 1995 by The Lockman Foundation. Used by permission (www.Lockman.org).

Scripture quotations marked NLT are taken from the *Holy Bible, New Living Translation*, copyright © 1996, 2004. Used by permission of Tyndale House Publishers, Inc., Wheaton, Illinois 60189, U.S.A. All rights reserved.

Italics in Scripture have been added by the author.

Editorial Services provided by the Livingstone Corp.

Published in association with Yates & Yates, LLP, Attorneys and Counselors, Orange, California.

Cover design: Brand Navigation, LLC

Cover image: istock

Interior design: Smartt Guys design

**Library of Congress Cataloging-in-Publication Data**

Ingram, Chip
  Holy ambition : turning God-shaped dreams into reality/ Chip Ingram.
    p. cm.
  ISBN 978-0-8024-2983-4
  1. Spiritual direction. 2. Christian life. 3. Bible. O.T. Nehemiah—Commentaries. I. Title.
  BV5053.I54 2010
  248.4—dc22
              2010009795

We hope you enjoy this book from Moody Publishers. Our goal is to provide high-quality, thought-provoking books and products that connect truth to your real needs and challenges. For more information on other books and products written and produced from a biblical perspective, go to www.moodypublishers.com or write to:

Moody Publishers
820 N. LaSalle Boulevard
Chicago, IL 60610


1 3 5 7 9 10 8 6 4 2

*Printed in the United States of America*

I dedicate this book

to all those whose lives God has used

to ignite holy ambition in my heart and life.

Chief among them is my wife, Theresa,

who has consistently modeled before me

the compassion of a dislocated heart,

the prayer life of a broken spirit,

and the unwavering sacrifice of a radical faith.

# contents

# foreword

When Chip Ingram sat in my classroom many years ago, my eyes and ears popped wide open with his perceptive questions, his heart that was obviously bursting with concern for people, and his warm, friendly gaze that etched out the profile of a young man with a promising postseminary ministry. He did not disappoint me. Now with his exceptional track record as pastor, radio teacher, and biblical counselor, Chip has put on paper his basic spiritual tool kit.

The Gallup poll commented some years ago that Americans had never before confessed to so much Christian activity yet making so little difference in how we live — clear evidence that thousands who have trusted Christ as Savior are shuffling along in hazy uncertainty. Like a calm voice from the control tower, Chip talks through the pages of *Holy Ambition* as though guiding a disoriented pilot down through the fog onto the landing strip. He writes intimately in the second person, to "you," because he knows the language of his generation. He speaks to the multitude of wanderers in the Christian wilderness — believers en route to heaven who are misusing valuable time and energy because they have no tracking system.

Six supporting girders from the Scriptures guide the reader toward God's safe haven: a heart, a spirit, a faith, a plan, a commitment, and a soul. From the lives of biblical standouts such as King Asa and the prophet Nehemiah, the book lifts up models. Here is how they did it; now you do it. There is no lofty theological language, although Chip's doctrinal underpinnings are clearly discernible. His pages are about quality of life, a book for activists who truly care about making their lives a booster rocket in the world instead of just another churchgoing cipher. There has never been a better time than now for such a strategic call to lighting our lamps in a dark world.

**Howard G. Hendricks**
*Distinguished Professor, Chairman*
*Center for Christian Leadership*
*Dallas Theological Seminary*

# introduction

Thank you!

By picking up this book and reading these words you have allowed me to spend some valuable moments with you. Believe me, I'm grateful for the opportunity. It's a rare privilege to revise and update this book with real stories and true accounts of how God has birthed and accomplished "Holy Ambition" from all kinds of people from all walks of life.

What is most exciting about this edition is not a change in the content, but the opportunity to let you hear from people like yourself who "longed to make a difference for God" and then learned how to turn that desire into action by reading this book.

You'll hear stories of stay-at-home moms who revolutionize their homes to corporate executives who are transforming the world. You'll learn how a woman with cancer turned her pain into a ministry to those undergoing chemotherapy in the city of Chicago. Seminary students and Bible college graduates have written and e-mailed to tell me how they discovered God's calling on their life through the biblical principles of this book.

It's not because I'm something special or have some insight that no one else has, but because it's true and it's from God's Word. And what He's done in my life and countless others, He wants to do in yours. If the truth in this book becomes the tool in your life that it has been in mine, it will show you that you can be a difference maker! You can actually be a tool in the hands of the eternal God of the universe to make an impact on your world! God can and will use you to accomplish His purposes in ways that will shock and delight you. Put simply, you can be a difference maker!

You may think making a difference is for extraordinary people. You may think that a life of adventure and excitement and being greatly used by God is for people who are smarter, more gifted, and know much more than you know. The fact of the matter is, that's simply not true. One of the greatest myths propagated in the church today is that God only uses superstars. No one comes out and says it, but it's what we all assume. We think God is going to use the bright, highly gifted, unique, and extraordinary individuals. But even a casual glance at the characters of the Bible reveals this to be a lie. Because we tend to talk about our heroes in Scripture in superficial ways, we make them bigger than life. We make them extra special and extraordinary. But the fact is, God has chosen very regular, ordinary, common people just like you and me to accomplish the biggest events in all of human history. He used a teenage girl to bring His Son into this planet. He used a blue-collar worker to raise Him from childhood and teach Him about a life of integrity and worship. He used common fishermen to lay the foundation for the greatest revolution that has ever touched the world. And God wants to use you and God wants to use me in the same ways.

This book is about how that happens.

This book is about moving beyond the status quo.

This book is about living beyond Christianity 101. It's about moving beyond what the Christian subculture tells us is right and holy and acceptable. It's about the truth we've lost—that the God of the universe is actually looking for ordinary people like you and me to accomplish things beyond our wildest dreams. It's about holy ambition!

What God is seeking, what He's looking for, are not the brightest and the best. God is looking for people who are willing to live on the edge. People who long to have a life of significance and impact. People who are willing to believe that what God has said is true and will step out in tiny incremental steps as God leads. People who will let God breathe into them dreams that can change the world. People who so long to see God's agenda fulfilled in this fallen world that they attempt what seems impossible, ridiculous, and "outside the box," for God's glory. People with holy ambition!

Now, lest you get the wrong idea, this is not about becoming visible, famous, or necessarily being in the limelight. Some of the greatest men and women of God will never be known this side of eternity. They've worked behind the scenes. They've done things that only God knows about, but they've been used to transform their world. So it's not about what other people think.

It's about being fully supported by an all-powerful, all-knowing God who will do in and through you exceedingly, abundantly beyond your wildest imagination. It's about living on the edge. It's about an adventure of faith—breaking through the sludge and stagnation that characterize so much of the Christian faith in our day. It's about holy ambition!

## WHAT DOES IT TAKE?

Depending on how you have responded to what you have read so far, you likely fall into one of four groups:

**Group One** is seriously considering closing the book with a sigh and a sad conclusion: "This isn't for me. I can't relate to holy ambition. God hasn't and probably can't use me."

**Group Two** is filled with personal questions: "Is God looking for me? Could I really be a person God would use? Could I actually be part of something great and exciting? How?"

**Group Three** already has a checklist of practical questions started: "All right, Chip, what's it going to take? How can I be sure these principles work? How much time are we talking about here? Where do I start?"

**Group Four** has been nodding with deep understanding. You know you're making a difference, but you're also experiencing frustrations. You're not sure exactly how you've been effective because you've been functioning by spiritual intuition. You have a difficult time describing the process to others or walking through the steps with them. You're ready for some help and encouragement!

I'll let you in on a secret. Whichever one of these groups you fit into right now, you are already showing one or more of the spiritual signs God is looking for. This gift may not be showing up in exactly the right place and it may need to be refocused, but I can assure you that you already have part of what it takes to be the kind of person God is seeking. But I'm getting a little ahead of the plan here.

First, I have some questions for you, no matter which group comes closest to describing you. Each of these groups represents a certain spiritual condition that all Christians face at one time or another. My question is this: Have you decided to settle into the group that described your present condition?

**You in Group One:** Have you basically given up on God, or are you willing to consider that God might have a bigger plan for you than you can see or imagine right now?

**You in Group Two:** Will you just live with your doubts, fears, and questions, or will you trust that God can show Himself amazingly faithful if you give Him an opportunity?

**You in Group Three:** You are eager to get started, but are you willing to let God help you count what it will cost you to live on the edge with Him? Are you willing to temporarily slow down those internal RPMs of activity to allow God to work more deeply in you so He can work more powerfully through you?

**You in Group Four:** Please don't give up! Help from God's Word is on the way. He's already started a good work in you. Are you willing to allow God's wisdom to help you clarify what He has already done in and through you?

The way you answered these questions will indicate whether or not a seed of holy ambition is already planted in you. You want something more in your Christian life. You want your life to make a difference for God. You want to experience, in a deep and unmistakable way, exactly what Jesus meant when He announced, "I came that they may have life, and have it abundantly" (John 10:10 NASB). You know you have *life* in Christ—that's a gift! What you are hungry for is the *abundantly* part. You are really fed up with being part of a Christianity that claims to be alive but appears sluggish at best. You are tired of being part of a Christianity that claims to be life transforming but too often looks like nothing more than a religious subculture that promises much but delivers little.

It's time for holy ambition. It's time for Christians to live like Christians. For a church that shakes the world. For a people of God who make a difference. It's time for us to be what God wants: people who will let Him do a powerful work in them and through them!

Could this really happen? Yes it can and it is today! It *is* happening! God is doing extraordinary things through ordinary people. I want to tell you about other people like you—not superstars, but people who have seen God do mighty things in and through them. People who have an intensity to their faith and a spiritual passion I call "holy ambition." *People who have discovered what it takes to make a difference for God.*

These pages will introduce you to the components of holy ambition. In order for your life to make a significant difference for God, He will take you through six incremental steps that will prepare you and engage you in His service. They are, in order of experience:

Developing a **Dislocated Heart**
Experiencing a **Broken Spirit**
Practicing a **Radical Faith**
Creating a **Strategic Plan**
Exercising **Personal Commitment**
Growing a **Courageous Soul**

Each of these will be explained and illustrated from Scripture, particularly from the life of one man, Nehemiah. These six developmental phases represent essential and unavoidable components to a life of holy ambition. As you study them (and experience them), you will learn to look at life in a very different way. You will come to understand the value Jesus places on your life. Holy ambition will give you a new perspective on what Jesus meant when He said, "For whoever wishes to save his life will lose it; *but whoever loses his life for My sake will find it*" (Matthew 16:25 NASB).

## A PRAYER FOR OUR JOURNEY TOGETHER

Holy Father, teach us to burn white hot with ambition and great dreams that are God-given and grace-induced. Make us ambitious for Your agenda and Your glory. Use us to bring hope and life and relief from suffering in ways beyond our wildest dreams. And yet, throughout this journey, do an even deeper work within our hearts. Sanctify us. Grant us pure motives. And help us, every step of the journey, to long to please You more than impress people.

O Holy Father, give us holy ambition!

Lord, we want to change our world and honor You, but we fear we will do it in our own strength, in our own flesh, and do it to meet our personal needs.

O Holy Father, give us holy ambition!

Even as we long to make an impact, we also long for comfort and peace. We're tempted to stay where it seems safe even though we know that our only real security comes only from You. We long for significance, but we fear stepping out to make a difference.

O Holy Father, give us holy ambition.

## HOW TO ENRICH YOUR EXPERIENCE

In recent years thousands of people have gone through this material. From the feedback and stories we have received, a consistent theme has been that going through this material in a group has been a transformational experience. So, not only have we revised the content of the book, we have also created a small group video curriculum to go along with the book. In these brief but engaging video sessions, Chip will challenge and encourage your group. You can order a copy of this small group DVD by going to www.livingontheedge.org.

*"Well done, good and faithful servant!"*

MATTHEW 25:21

# holy
# AMBITION

You have probably heard the phrase, "Well done, good and faithful servant!" as long as you have been a Christian. You may even know that Jesus used the phrase twice in one of His parables (Matthew 25:21, 23) to give us a picture of the way God will settle accounts at the end of the age. I'm sure you have heard at least one sermon that ended with an emotional appeal to think about how wonderful it would be in eternity to stand before God and hear Him say, "Well done, good and faithful servant." The problem is such sermons rarely tell you what it will take to get there.

Most Christians I talk to want to finish well. Unfortunately, "finishing well" gets translated into some vague wish that God will say something nice to them in eternity, but they don't dare make that phrase the purpose of their lives. But if that isn't the purpose for living once we've met Christ, then what is? What is the target of our Christian life? If we aim at nothing, we're sure to hit it. What are we aiming at as we follow Christ? What's our holy ambition? What do we really want God to say to us someday?

I know *ambition* is one of those almost forbidden words in Christian circles. It shares a place with words like *discipline, suffering, passion,* and *perseverance* on a list of terms that may offend comfortable Christians or skittish pagans. Based on our sensitivities, the Bible is full of such offensive language. It calls us sinners and questions our integrity. If we weren't dealing with God's Word, we might resent the insinuations. The New International Version uses the word *ambition* seven times. Five uses are negative (selfish ambition) and two are positive. Paul told the Romans, "It has always been my ambition to preach the gospel where Christ was not known, so that I would not be building on someone else's foundation" (Romans 15:20). He also told the Thessalonians, "Make it your ambition to lead a quiet life" (1 Thessalonians 4:11a). Other translations tend to substitute the word *aspiration* for *ambition*, but I like the edginess of *holy ambition.* That's because I find the attitude of holy ambition taught everywhere in Scripture. It's unavoidable. The phrase itself isn't used that often, but many commands and directions from God's Word can only be applied if we make them our holy ambition. Consider these examples:

> Trust in the Lord with all your heart and do not lean on your own understanding.
> In all your ways acknowledge Him, and He will make your paths straight.
> —**PROVERBS 3:5–6** NASB

> But it is not this way with you, but the one who is the greatest among you
> must become like the youngest, and the leader like the servant. For who is greater,
> the one who reclines at the table or the one who serves? Is it not the one who
> reclines at the table? But I am among you as the one who serves. You are those who
> have stood by Me in My trials; and just as My Father has granted Me a
> kingdom, I grant you that you may eat and drink at My table in My kingdom,

> **Holy ambition is deep and long. It affects every part of life for all of life.**

and you will sit on thrones judging the twelve tribes of Israel.

—LUKE 22:26–30 NASB

And He was saying to them all, "If anyone wishes to come after Me, he must deny himself, and take up his cross daily and follow Me. For whoever wishes to save his life will lose it, but whoever loses his life for My sake, he is the one who will save it."

—LUKE 9:23–24 NASB

What you just read is only a sample. Each passage presupposes or demands that we respond with holy ambition. If we make it our ambition to save our lives, Jesus said, we will lose them. But if we make it our holy ambition to lose our lives for His sake, Jesus promises that we will discover and experience life to its fullest.

Holy ambition is deep and long. It affects every part of life for all of life. The depth and length of our holy ambition will be tested. Those who prove faithful will hear God say someday, "Well done, good and faithful servant!"

## THE STARTING PLACE

Right here at the start of our journey, things get tricky. How does holy ambition actually work? Is this just another book about trying harder, getting up earlier, and praying more? How does holy ambition turn into a life that makes a difference? What's my part? What's God's part? The landscape around holy ambition can be very dangerous unless we understand how God creates and sustains this passion in our hearts. God wants to do something supernatural and tremendous through you; but unless you understand where He begins and how He works, you're destined for failure.

That's why one Old Testament verse has had particular meaning to me over the last twenty-five years. I memorized this verse when I first became a Christian but didn't understand its full impact. The words simply struck me as too wonderful to be true. Later, as I studied this passage carefully, I came to understand that this was not only a promise for one king in Israel but also a timeless axiom of how God relates to every man and every woman in every age. Follow along carefully and listen to the spirit behind these words:

For the eyes of the Lord move to and fro throughout the earth that He may
strongly support those whose heart is completely His.

—2 CHRONICLES 16:9A NASB

Please read this statement again *slowly*. Think of it as true, not just something written three thousand years ago in the land of Israel but at this very moment in your life, your neighborhood, and your church. This verse expresses not some antiquated view of God but a timeless truth. It describes the omniscient (all-knowing), all-powerful, all-wise God who is carefully considering the earth and looking for a select group of people. As you read this verse, are you among those people whose hearts are fully His? The promise of this amazing passage is that God is actually looking for people He can strongly support. In other words, God wants to do far more in most all of us than most of us want Him to do. He is looking today for something in the human heart that will ignite His support in his or her life.

## God Seeks People Who Are Completely His

## What Kind of People Does God Seek?
## (Completely His)

Nothing hides from God. Every covering and shelter becomes transparent under His knowing glance. He sees through high-priced and low-rent walls. No skin color deflects His gaze. He could see right through us, but our Creator adjusts His view to consider one part of who we are — our hearts. God looks for a select group of hearts found in widely differing people throughout the world. This select group never has race, income, education, culture, intelligence, charisma, or style in common. What they share is a heart that completely belongs to God. Their hearts beat with holy ambition.

When the ancient prophet Hanani described God to King Asa, he was merely stating what God had done, was doing, and would always do in every place and in all times. God looks for a select group of people whose hearts are completely His. That's what Hanani meant when he said, "For the eyes of the

Lord move to and fro throughout the earth that He may strongly support those whose heart is completely His" (2 Chronicles 16:9 NASB). God is doing that right now. The question is: Where are you? For a moment, follow God's eyes into your own being. What do you think He sees? Does His all-knowing look find a heart in you that belongs completely to Him?

The New Living Translation of this verse says that God looks for a man or a woman or a student or a child whose heart is "fully committed to him." These are people who, when they hear the call of God directing them to do this or that, leap to obey. They may have emotional struggles, just as you and I do. They may not enjoy a particular act of obedience. They may not feel like obeying. They struggle with the implications, relationships, finances, and geography that obedience to God always involves, but they do what He has asked. High cost? They do it. Complications? They do it. Repercussions? They do it. They make a difference. They change the world. In ways you may not even know, your life has been deeply affected by people whose hearts have been completely God's. God has built His kingdom, and He builds His church on that kind of people.

Are you that kind of person? Do you have a heart that belongs to God and do you want to live on the edge? Are you ready to take the steps that develop holy ambition? Maybe you honestly don't know. Fair enough. Are you willing to find out? If you are, then these chapters will help you.

## A KING'S HEART

In order to better understand what it means to have a heart completely God's, let's begin by looking briefly at the life of a man who had holy ambition, but faltered. This is not a story with a happy ending. Although King Asa's heart began in the right place, he eventually backed away from the life God offered him. That's when God sent the prophet Hanani to speak to King Asa the words we have already seen: "For the eyes of the Lord move to and fro throughout the earth that He may strongly support those whose heart is completely His" (2 Chronicles 16:9 NASB). People who are familiar with that verse are often shocked to discover its context. The verse comes with a story. Without the story, the verse loses much of its punch. For, although the prophet was describing God's ways, he was not describing the king's heart.

## Early Years

You can read the summary of Asa's life in 2 Chronicles 14–16. God showed Asa how pleased He was with the king's early dependency, faith, and courage. The first ten years of his reign were conducted under peaceful conditions. Since his borders were secure, Asa decided to take on building projects. He gave God credit for the peace and began to develop new cities and construct fortified walls around existing ones. Rising towers and gates pushed consumer confidence to new heights. The people enjoyed a time of great prosperity.

## A Time for War

Suddenly, around year ten, a looming cloud of uncertainty overshadowed the bright economic forecast for Judah. An army almost twice the size of Asa's approached from the southwest. This was a major reality check for the king and his people. Within his borders, Asa had passed the early test of his leadership by taking a stand for God. Prosperity followed. Now it was time for another test.

Faced with impossible odds, Asa did a very wise thing. He turned to God. "Then Asa called to the Lord his God and said, 'Lord, there is no one like you to help the powerless against the mighty. Help us, O Lord our God, for we rely on you, and in your name we have come against this vast army. O Lord, you are our God; do not let man prevail against you" (2 Chronicles 14:11). Asa put his kingdom and his future in God's hands.

God's answer was immediate, swift, and decisive: "The Lord struck down the Cushites before Asa and Judah. The Cushites fled" (2 Chronicles 14:12). Huge success. The army carried lots of loot and livestock back to Jerusalem. A great disaster was averted, but had any lessons been learned? Time would tell.

## The Promise and the Warning

Shortly after the victory, the prophet Azariah came to Asa and basically said, "King, it has been a long time since God has been so honored, and you are moving in the right direction. Asa, God wants you to consider a proposition. Here it is. If you will trust and obey Him, and your people will trust and obey Him, He will be with you and He will do things beyond what you ever dreamed. But if you forsake Him, He will forsake you."

Asa took the prophet's words to heart and put them into action. The lands of Judah, Benjamin, and the surrounding territories got a thorough idol-cleansing. The altar for sacrifices to God in front of the temple in Jerusalem was repaired and put back into service. A revival of worship and obedience broke out in the nation that peaked in the fifteenth year of Asa's reign. People pledged allegiance to Yahweh and turned away from their sins. The Scriptures describe the attitude of king and people in this way: *"They sought God eagerly, and he was found by them.* So the Lord gave them rest on every side" (2 Chronicles 15:15).

The land experienced another time of great blessing. For the next twenty years, Asa reigned and walked with God. He trusted the Lord. The years flew by. Life in the kingdom of Judah settled into the kind of routine that usually precedes another test. The king and the people were well, feeling settled, but they were about to discover that life with God doesn't involve "settling." Holy ambition is not a permanent condition. It's not about dramatic, one-time decisions, or living off our faith from the past. It involves active trust and continuous obedience. It's all about living on the edge, living now!

### A Test of Holy Ambition

Thirty-five years into his reign, Asa was suddenly faced with a new challenge. A coalition of enemies surrounded Judah. Asa did something he hadn't done in thirty-five years. Until this point, he had an unblemished record. Now, instead of trusting God, he decided to handle this problem on his own.

Asa's determination to trust God and be a difference maker had been dulled by twenty years of peace and financial prosperity. His years of success had gradually hardened his heart and shifted his focus from God to himself.

So God brought a new test to Asa to give him another opportunity to succeed. But instead of trusting God, he emptied the treasury, contacted one of Israel's powerful allies, paid him off, and got his help to defeat the Israelites. Strategically, politically, and militarily, all this was a brilliant move. Spiritually, it meant disaster for Asa. He soon got another visit from a prophet. That visit is the context of the underlying theme of this book.

Hanani came to Asa king of Judah and said to him, *"Because you relied on the king of Aram and not on the Lord your God, the army of the king of Aram has escaped from your hand"* (2 Chronicles 16:7). Then Hanani reminded him, "Were not the Cushites and Libyans a mighty army with great numbers of chariots and horsemen? *Yet when you relied on the Lord,* he delivered them into your hand" (2 Chronicles 16:8). Now comes our theme verse: "For the eyes of the Lord move to and fro throughout the earth that He may strongly support those whose heart is completely His" (2 Chronicles 16:9 NASB). But there's more. Here's the end of that verse that most people don't quote: "You have done a foolish thing, and from now on you will be at war" (2 Chronicles 16:9).

### The Moment of Truth

This turning point in Asa's reign would determine whether he would renew his commitment to holy ambition or step away from God's guidance. The moment provides an amazing applicational insight for us. Here was a man who had walked with God for at least thirty-five years. An unexpected crisis caught him off guard, and he made a serious error in judgment. Then he had to listen to God's prophet call him a fool. But instead of repenting, Asa reacted in anger toward Hanani and threw him in prison. Now there's a wise and godly move!

Unfortunately, the king wasn't through being foolish. He brutally oppressed some of his people. He turned his back on holy ambition. He leaned away from God instead of toward Him. His effectiveness faded. Within five years, Asa developed a serious disease in his feet. He still didn't admit his foolishness or ask God for help. He died in the forty-first year of his reign.

We look at Asa's life and see great success. Each of the apparent difficulties God brought across Asa's path turned out to be a door of opportunity until that event in year thirty-five. After that failure, God had some direct words for the king. He basically said, "If you had trusted Me as you did before, I would have taken care of everything! Israel and that even bigger enemy you paid off by emptying the treasury were no problem for Me. I would have taken care of all of them. You know why, Asa? Because what was true when you were desperate and young in the faith remains true today: The eyes of the Lord still go to and fro throughout the whole earth. Why? Because I want to support every man, every woman, every student whose heart is fully committed to Me." Asa missed a golden opportunity. We are left with the sad record of someone who did not end nearly as well as he started.

## WHAT ABOUT YOUR STORY?

How do you think your life will end? For a moment, picture your life as a time continuum on which you mark the point when you came to Christ. I sincerely hope you are already part of God's family. Where are you right now? How far have you moved from your starting point with Christ? Where do you think you will be when your life ends? What kind of commentary would God write for you up to this point? Does your life look more like the early years of Asa or more like the latter years? Those are penetrating questions, aren't they?

There's at least one important principle from Asa's life I don't want you to miss. Past success (faith, and dependency on God) is no guarantee of future faithfulness. In fact, as I read the pages of the Old and New Testament, I find very few men and very few women who ended well. Few heroes ended heroically. Few runners crossed the finish line as winners. Beyond Scripture I've noticed the same sad pattern. Many Christians coast or fade badly at the end of their race. They start well, but they usually finish poorly. There are not many churches that start well, grow, and then stay well.

> *Our focus is primarily on the rearview mirror — what God did in our past — instead of radically trusting Him for the future.*

Do you know what usually happens with people, churches, and organizations—people like you and like me? Once we experience success because we trusted God out of desperation, we usually go on to do one of two things: (1) we take the success and its results for granted and become arrogant, or (2) we forget the process God used and settle into a comfort zone that leaves God in a corner of our lives. Survival tactics gradually replace holy ambition. We get respectable inside Christian circles and gradually come to resist the idea that faith has anything to do with risk.

We may proclaim our security in Christ even though we are actually relying on every other form of security than Christ. We avoid risk. Our focus is primarily on the rearview mirror—what God did in our past—instead of radically trusting Him for the future. We learn to depend on people, on laws, on principles. We begin to level off or settle down, losing any sense of holy ambition, losing sight of the edge, that close reliance on God.

Life flies by, just like it did for Asa.

Then, after a while, God brings another test. And now we fail in battles whose victory God guarantees. Like Asa, in spite of all God's promises and resources, we make decisions that snatch defeat out of the jaws of victory. We end poorly. That's a lesson from the pages of Scripture mirrored in lives today.

I don't know about you, but I don't want my life in Christ to end poorly. I don't want that for my family or for the church I lead. And I don't want that for you. But honestly, I fear that history tells me the odds are against us. The only way I know to beat the odds is find a God-given holy ambition and allow that to shape my life.

## FINDING HOLY AMBITION

When we're talking about holy ambition, we are talking about answering God's call. Looking at lives like Asa's certainly jars us out of complacency and awakens our spiritual concern. But that's not enough. We need to spend time studying and imitating those who did run the race all the way. We need some real heroes, and God has provided them in people like Nehemiah. In the pages to come, we will take a close look at his life.

God calls us to holy ambition, not only individually, but also corporately. You can't live on the edge without getting other people involved. Holy ambition is selectively contagious. Some will follow your example; others won't. That, as we will see, is all part of the joy and challenge of living powerfully for God.

Holy ambition means living with a large purpose in life. I like to remind our church regularly of our particular challenge with this question: Are we going to answer God's call for this church to make a significant impact in this new millennium, or will we rest on past success? Can you personalize that challenge?

## How will you answer God's call on your life to be a difference maker while you walk this earth?

What will it take to really make a difference for God? The rest of this book is designed to help you answer that question. And in it you will learn the six conditions that God looks for in the lives of people He uses:

- A dislocated heart
- A broken spirit
- A radical faith
- A strategic plan
- A personal commitment
- A courageous soul

These conditions hold true if you are married, single, old or young, rich or poor. They apply to laymen, pastors, missionaries, and businessmen. They are conditions that transcend age, gender, race, or cultural background. If you are a business, small group, or church leader, I have included a small group study that follows a brief DVD presentation that will help you pursue holy ambition as a group. But remember, when the eyes of the Lord are searching the earth, He is primarily looking for starting points, for individual men and women who will be catalysts for change that draw others into lives of holy ambition for God.

The first thing God notes when He finds a select person who is moving toward holy ambition is a dislocated heart. That's the best place for us to start, too. Do you have a dislocated heart?

## TALK IT OVER

**Question from Chip on the video:** *If God gave you an unlimited check to do anything for Him, what is the desire that is on your heart?*

**1.** How would you define "holy ambition"?

**2.** For you personally, what would it look like to "finish well"? What would need to be true of you so that God would say, "well done, good and faithful servant"?

**3.** "For the eyes of the Lord move to and fro throughout the earth that He may strongly support those whose heart is completely His" (2 Chronicles 16:9a).

   What is your greatest roadblock to having a heart that is "completely His"?

**4.** When in your life were you most living "all out" for Christ?

**5.** Spend some time talking about the following words from the lips of Jesus. What do these verses teach us about "holy ambition"?

*As they were walking along the road, a man said to him, "I will follow you wherever you go." Jesus replied, "Foxes have holes and birds of the air have nests, but the Son of Man has no place to lay his head." He said to another man, "Follow me." But the man replied, "Lord, first let me go and bury my father." Jesus said to him, "Let the dead bury their own dead, but you go and proclaim the kingdom of God." Still another said, "I will follow you, Lord; but first let me go back and say good-by to my family." Jesus replied, "No one who puts his hand to the plow and looks back is fit for service in the kingdom of God."* **Luke 9:57–62 (NIV)**

**6.** Chip said that Asa's determination to be "a difference maker had been dulled by twenty years of peace and financial prosperity." What is in your life that can dull your holy ambition?

**7.** Who do you respect and admire as someone who "finished well"? It could be someone in Scripture or a personal acquaintance. What is it about their life that you respect the most?

## LIVE IT OUT

**1.** Connect this week with someone whose heart seems to be "completely God's." Have a spiritual conversation about life and faith. Learn from them what they do to keep their "edge" spiritually.

**2.** This week read for yourself the story of Asa from 2 Chronicles 14–16 and answer the following two questions.

| Where do you see holy ambition in Asa's life? | Where do you see selfish ambition in Asa's life? |
|---|---|

To order a copy of the small group video curriculum taught by Chip, go to www.livingontheedge.org. These brief but engaging video sessions will both encourage and challenge your group.

*"For the eyes of the Lord move to and fro throughout the earth that He may strongly support those whose heart is completely His."*

—2 CHRONICLES 16:9 NASB

# 2

# a dislocated
# HEART

the first condition in developing holy ambition

___

L et me guess what you are thinking right now. *Dislocated heart? What's that? Why on earth would I want to develop a dislocated heart, Chip? It sounds awkward, uncomfortable, and maybe even painful. I mean, I've heard of dislocated shoulders, dislocated fingers, and dislocated toes, and I don't particularly want any of those. Can you give me one good reason (or two) why I would want a dislocated heart? Or better yet, why God would want me to have one?*

The short answer to that question is that God uses a dislocated heart as a foundation for accomplishing His will. Holy ambition begins with a dislocated heart. So how do you get one? Our mentor for this lesson is Nehemiah, a king's cupbearer turned city renovator.

## NEHEMIAH'S DISLOCATED HEART

Nehemiah's story begins with a historical hint and a spiritual hurt. It was a time when God's people and God's agenda in the world seemed hopelessly lost while Nehemiah lived in the lap of luxury. Here are the opening verses:

> The words of Nehemiah son of Hacaliah:
> In the month of Kislev in the twentieth year, while I was in the citadel of Susa, Hanani, one of my brothers, came from Judah with some other men, and I questioned them about the Jewish remnant that survived the exile, and also about Jerusalem.
> They said to me, "Those who survived the exile and are back in the province are in great trouble and disgrace. The wall of Jerusalem is broken down, and its gates have been burned with fire."
> When I heard these things, I sat down and wept. For some days I mourned and fasted and prayed before the God of heaven.
>
> NEHEMIAH 1:1–4

I hope you can imagine this scene. Nehemiah was living in the king's palace, surrounded by servants and satisfied with fine food, luxurious benefits, and economic security. Then came the terrible report from Jerusalem. Nehemiah's brother and others had returned from Jerusalem, where they had journeyed to see the conditions in the city. They brought back news that broke Nehemiah's heart. How do we know? Because he sat down and wept.

*A dislocated heart is not simply a strong emotional response or a gush of sadness over bad news.*

Let's get this clear in our minds. Nehemiah's life was going great, but God's agenda in Jerusalem was stalled. Nehemiah was blessed while God's city was in ruins. His response to the news was a dislocated heart. Even though his spiritual life was in order and the conditions in Jerusalem did not directly affect his personal world, Nehemiah's deeper concern for God's agenda caused his heart to break when he heard the report.

How do you react to bad news? How do you deal with those times when something is going on in the world that threatens your way of life or what you're comfortable with? When was the last time you prayed, mourned, and fasted after hearing a report about God's will not being fulfilled in His church? I mean that literally. When was the last time you wept after news about the plight of people in need? When was the last time you were emotionally, even viscerally, disturbed when you heard about injustice, suffering, or God's people operating in a way that was contrary to the clear, written will of God?

These questions aren't meant to shame us. They are meant to move us to seriously consider God's purposes in our lives. My experience is that when most of us hear disturbing news, we try to get quick closure. We try to explain, deny, or painlessly supply the need—anything that will avoid a strong, long, or draining demand on the way we want to live. Actually, what we try desperately to avoid is having our hearts dislocated. We don't want to be disturbed by someone else's problems. Those tendencies are what make Nehemiah's reactions to news from a faraway place so powerful and remarkable. His dislocated heart was the first condition that led to the amazing work God did in and through his life.

Nehemiah certainly responded to the report he heard. Don't miss the details. But a dislocated heart is not simply a strong emotional response or a gush of sadness over bad news. It is not simply a knee-jerk reaction to an overwhelming need. No, from time clues later in the book, we know that Nehemiah grieved and prayed for four months. This wasn't a "flash in the pan" emotional experience. This took time. He fasted, prayed, and met with God.

## NEHEMIAH'S SITUATION

Before we look closely at Nehemiah's prayer, let me give you some background that may help you understand his response and actions. Nehemiah was a Jewish cupbearer to Artaxerxes, king of the Persians. His employment was part of the long-term by-product of God's punishment of Israel and Judah. You will remember from Old Testament history that God's people insisted on worshiping idols. God had already established the rule that idolatry would lead to humiliation, defeat, and captivity. In about 722 BC, God allowed the

Assyrians to conquer the ten tribes of Israel and ship them off as slaves. Then, in 586 BC, the Babylonians took Judah into captivity.

During the years that followed, while Daniel was in captivity, the Babylonians were taken over by the Persians. The new world-superpower reversed many of the policies of the Babylonians, and a couple of groups of Jews returned to Judah. Zerubbabel led an exile band back to rebuild the temple. That occurred in about 536. Nearly eighty years later, in approximately 458, Ezra returned to Jerusalem to teach the people who were there, but by then, few exiles were interested in returning to the Promised Land.

Nehemiah's account begins in the twentieth year of Artaxerxes, the Persian king. Seventy years had passed since the rebuilding of the temple in Jerusalem. Although the Jews were living in exile in Persia, the businesses they owned there were doing well. They had outlived their status as prisoners of war, and many thought of themselves as immigrants. The Jewish kids liked it in Persia, and a lot of them didn't even speak their traditional language of Hebrew. A few faithful people had gone back with Ezra to keep the dream of the Promised Land alive, but they are not doing well.

Meanwhile, Nehemiah found himself in a prestigious position as a royal cupbearer. He tasted the wine and food prepared for the king. The role had at least as much peril as prestige. Usually, a foreigner was trained as a cupbearer, because rulers didn't trust someone from their own clan. Many kings were assassinated by food poisoning. So it was common to identify a trustworthy person who not only would taste the king's food but become a royal sounding board. Cupbearers were often a king's closest confidants.

So as long as no one spiked the royal stew, Nehemiah had it made. He wore the best clothes, rode in the best chariot, and enjoyed a life of comfort. His life shows us that he was a man of order, contentment, and success. He probably had a condo in the palace. Nehemiah must have been tempted at times to forget his roots and adopt the Persian lifestyle.

Yet, hundreds of miles away, events were unfolding that would complicate Nehemiah's life and dislocate his heart. His Jewish brothers in Jerusalem were discouraged and disgraced. The walls of the city were still in ruins. The gates remained charred and useless from previous defeats. Enemies made regular raids. The people were disheartened. God's agenda seemed to have been permanently thwarted.

Although God had promised that He would rebuild Jerusalem and regather His people, almost a hundred and fifty years had passed since the Babylonians had sacked Jerusalem. God had said that He would do a great thing throughout Israel, but so little remained. When Nehemiah heard all this, he knew things were not going the right way. The news broke his heart.

## A DISLOCATED HEART

From these glimpses of Nehemiah's life we get the first prerequisite for being the kind of person God is going to use—a dislocated heart. The condition affects your life and then the world. That's what the news from the Promised Land revealed in Nehemiah: his dislocated heart.

Nehemiah's condition was a rare and wonderful part of God's plan. His work and his body were in Persia, but his heart was in Jerusalem. His heart was with God's agenda. His heart was with his people, who were hurting and needy.

Do you realize how rare that is? Have you noticed how deeply rooted we become in a safe set of expectations? How dependent our hearts are on our way of life? When things are going well for us—we can pay our bills, we have cars that run, we live in safe neighborhoods, we have steady jobs, our families are pretty much intact, and no one has a life-threatening disease—life is good!

*How many of us know the top three needs that are affecting the neighborhood in which we live?*

Oh, of course, we have some hardships and struggles and emotional ups and downs, but for most of us, when things are going well, we gradually become desensitized to the needs around us. How many of us have gone to Haiti or Mexico or the Middle East on a short-term mission trip and become acutely aware of the devastating needs around the world? How often have we viewed a late-night advertisement for World Vision or Compassion International, when our defenses were down, and felt a pang in our hearts and the need to do something to make a difference? How many of us know the top three needs that are affecting the neighborhood in which we live?

We all know that the problems of the world are overwhelming and that we can't change everything. But what can occur in the light of that knowledge is desensitization to the very real needs to which God may want us to respond. We look at today's headlines and complain that they are so negative. But unless we find a personal way to respond, we will get dulled to the desperation, aching needs, and tragedies to which God calls our attention. Instead, these become issues for other people, in other lands, with greater resources, to resolve. Yet, to make a difference for God, we must allow Him to deeply move us. We need to identify a personal connection with God's agenda in the world. We need to develop a dislocated heart.

Every great movement of God and every project that has brought about relief of human need and the fulfillment of God's will has started with one man or one woman who cared deeply enough to hear God's voice and stepped out to do something. It started with a dislocated heart. That person understood that he couldn't change everything, but he was convinced he had to change something!

## PROFILE OF A DISLOCATED HEART

What is a dislocated heart? *It is a God-given concern that propels us beyond our comfortable routine. It is a passionate concern for God's people and God's agenda that supersedes our own personal comfort and prosperity.* Nehemiah cared about things elsewhere when circumstances didn't dictate he had to.

Lest you think this concept of a dislocated heart is simply an isolated case from the Old Testament, let me give you two examples of dislocated hearts from the pages of the New Testament. The apostle Paul, in Romans 9, made a statement that I still can't get my arms around. It reflects one of the most dislocated hearts I've ever heard of. He wrote:

> I speak the truth in Christ—I am not lying, my conscience confirms
> it in the Holy Spirit—I have great sorrow and unceasing anguish in my heart.
> For I could wish that I myself were cursed and cut off from Christ for the
> sake of my brothers, those of my own race, the people of Israel.
>
> ROMANS 9:1–4

He was saying, "Lord, if I could lose my salvation and every Jewish brother come to know You, I wouldn't hesitate to make the trade."

I don't know about you, but I haven't had that kind of dislocated heart very many times in my life. But I have had occasions when I have taken a walk around the block slowly and looked at all the cars and the houses and the little kids, and instead of thinking, as I often have, about the stuff of their lives, I have asked myself, "I wonder if they really know God?"

Have you ever had that experience of looking over the cubicles at work or driving by the cars backed up on the highway and asking yourself, out loud, "How many of these people know about Christ? How many have been turned off by religion?" When you can't go to sleep at night, how often does your mind seriously ponder the question: How many people in my relational network know that Christ died for them and He loves them? How many times have you honestly asked, with the Spirit of God prompting your heart, "Do I really care about others? Do I give a rip? Does the way I use my time and money indicate that people really matter to me? Do my words indicate that I care?"

Or do you have to admit that living in our American culture you have, like me, become so desensitized that you can live your own little Christian life in your own little Christian world and never let the things that bother God bother you. The apostle Paul cared so much that he wanted to take the place of the lost.

If you think I might be pushing too hard on this, or that the apostle Paul might be some rare exception to the rule, let's look at the greatest dislocated heart in the entire universe. Our Savior Himself modeled for us the kind of heart He wants to develop inside each one of us. Note this amazing description:

> Your attitude should be the same as that of Christ Jesus:
> Who, being in very nature God,
> did not consider equality with God something to be grasped,
> but made himself nothing,
> taking the very nature of a servant,
> being made in human likeness.
> And being found in appearance as a man,

he humbled himself

and became obedient to death—

even death on a cross!

**PHILIPPIANS 2:5–8**

What was Jesus doing before He came to the earth? He was in the ultimate perfect setting. Angels, myriad angels, stood before the throne of God crying out, "Holy, Holy, Holy." Jesus willingly left heaven for earth and became a baby—fully God, fully flesh. He lived a perfect life. He revealed truth and grace. He was the innocent man who died on a cross for your sin and mine and everyone else's. Then He rose from the dead and empowered His church. His example models for us and compels us to get moving. Life is short. People are hurting. People are dying. And God wants to use you and me to make a difference in their lives.

Now, lest you think that having a dislocated heart means that you must necessarily become a missionary or accomplish some other large and noble task, think again. Stepping outside what's comfortable often begins with something very, very small. It's not about doing something great for God; it's about letting God do something great in your heart! God never does something great *through* us until He does something significant *in* us!

Remember that even the largest task for God starts with a small step. There are scores of families in our church who make sacrifices every week. They park in remote parking. They walk or take shuttles and gladly accept the inconvenience so that uncles, friends, neighbors, or visitors won't be hindered or discouraged by a full parking lot at church.

On a more personal note, I've learned that I need to constantly take "baby steps" out of my own comfort zone to keep my heart tender and open to what God wants to do in and through my life.

A few days ago while I was working out at 24 Hour Fitness, I noticed a middle-aged man with long gray hair and scores of tattoos. He was going strong when I got on the treadmill and after I got off. When I finished swimming laps, showering, and was ready to head home, he was soaking wet and still hard at it. I realized as I walked toward him that he was the kind of person who appeared to be wild, crazy, and maybe even dangerous. Everything in me wanted to withdraw when I sensed the Spirit of God prompting me to interact with him.

"Wow, you've really been going at it today," I said with my most confident and enthusiastic voice. "I really admire your discipline and intensity as I've watched you today," I added seeking to honestly affirm someone who looked like he was the "head honcho" of the Hell's Angels. What happened next floored me. He broke into a huge smile, extended his hand and said, "Thanks man, I really appreciate that." Within three minutes you would have thought we were old buddies. The wall of fear and suspicion evaporated. His external appearance faded into the background as I relearned you can't base an impression on outward appearance, and that every human being is longing to be honestly affirmed and cared about for who they are. These seemingly little incremental steps are how God grows people.

How about you? What steps have you taken recently that have been a stretch for you? What other steps might God want you to take? What small step of meeting someone else's need could really make a difference in his life and begin to cultivate in your own life the very thing God wants to do most? These small steps can be deciding to invite your neighbors over to dinner, introducing yourself to a stranger, letting someone go ahead of you in line at the bank or grocery store, or silently praying for those you don't know as you sit on a bench at a park or mall. But remember, the issue is not earning God's favor or simply serving other people; the issue is the cultivation of a heart that deeply cares about those other people you normally wouldn't care about.

> The issue is not earning God's favor or simply serving other people; the issue is the cultivation of a heart that deeply cares about those "other people" you normally wouldn't care about.

In fact, it is in the taking of these little steps that larger opportunities to grow our hearts will appear. I know families whose idea of a vacation is to pile everybody in a bus with other families and drive as many as nineteen hours, depending on the bus and traffic, to get to Mexico. They love little kids, so they give them food and clothes, and they build houses for the poor. And they develop more seriously dislocated hearts.

I pray for an epidemic of dislocated hearts. Everywhere I look I see what God does in and through dislocated hearts, and I'm overwhelmed. Most of the cutting-edge ministries I've been exposed to are the direct result of someone's dislocated heart. I know one man with a dislocated heart who has a gift of generosity. About fifteen years ago he came to me and said, "I have an inkling that God wants to use your teaching to help a lot more people than you might imagine." He paid for the whole first year of Living on the Edge's radio launch on a local station. A team of people joined him, bringing with them an awesome display of gifts and talents.

When two or three dislocated hearts are gathered in one place, look out! Who would have ever dreamed that one local station would grow into an international radio, television, and discipleship ministry? One man had a dislocated heart to reach the people in our immediate area. He was joined by a handful of others who dreamed of taking the message to all of California and then the world. Little did we know that fifteen years later millions of people would be listening and watching the teaching ministry of LOTE throughout America, in Russian- and Arabic-speaking countries, as well as multiple other countries around the globe. All because one man had a dislocated heart that spurred others to join him.

Now we hear reports on a daily basis of marriages that are being reconciled, of people who are coming to Christ, of teenagers who listen to the program, of pastors who take the material to use in their own churches to equip people for ministry. You see, you never know what God is going to do with a dislocated heart, but that is where it all begins.

## DEVELOPING A DISLOCATED HEART

How do you develop a dislocated heart? What can you do to prepare yourself for God's work in your life? *The process involves four specific actions.*

### 1. Honest, Personal Self-Evaluation

The apostle Paul gave the Colossians a dislocating command: "Since, then, you have been raised with Christ, *set your hearts on things above*, where Christ is seated at the right hand of God" (Colossians 3:1). Dislocation creates a strong drawing or pulling action. Wherever your heart is located, that's the direction you will move. If we "set our hearts on things above," if we begin to look at life from God's perspective, everything else in life will tend to follow. A godly dislocated heart cares deeply about the same things that God cares about.

Jesus seems to have had this same process in mind when He said, "Do not store up for yourselves treasures on earth. . . . But store up for yourselves treasures in heaven. . . . For where your treasure is, there your heart will be also" (Matthew 6:19–21). Hearts and treasures have an amazing relationship in Scripture. If you want to know for certain where your heart really is, just follow the money. If we can identify our treasure, we can find our hearts. We've got Jesus' word on that.

So if our hearts are located in the treasures and the safe zones of this world, they need to be relocated (or dislocated) to the treasures of heaven and God's presence (God's zone, if you will). If we know we haven't "set our hearts on things above," we can ask God to do that work in us. Let me give you a few questions that I regularly ask myself as I seek to evaluate the condition of my heart:

- Do I really care for the people around me each day? What's the evidence?

- Am I so wrapped up in the details of my life that other people are interruptions rather than opportunities to serve Christ? What needs to change?

- Does it matter to me what's happening in other places in the world? Have I become desensitized to the pain and suffering all around me? Unfortunately, the answer for most of us is yes. When all our excuses and rationalizations are pushed aside, most of us have to admit we simply don't care enough to do something. But a dislocated heart responds.

The first step toward developing a dislocated heart involves honestly examining your heart condition. Only you, God, and the Holy Spirit can do that.

*2. Genuine Repentance*

*Repentance* is a word you don't hear much these days. The word means "to change one's mind." It is also associated with deep feelings of sorrow or remorse. To put it simply, it means that we see our lack of a dislocated heart as an affront to God and a condition that brings great sorrow to His heart. Genuine repentance brings a shattering realization: I have often unconsciously been squeezed into the mold of my culture. I have begun to think as a consumer instead of a Christian. I have neglected the clear teaching of God's Word that commands me, "Do not conform any longer to the pattern of this world, but be transformed by the renewing of your mind. Then you will be able to test and approve what God's will is—his good, pleasing and perfect will" (Romans 12:2).

Repentance may be a painful process to go through, but it is necessary. It is painful because we see ourselves in a light we've never seen ourselves in before. Let me give you a quick picture of what repentance will look like and what it will mean as you ask God to give you a dislocated heart.

Genuine repentance means that we admit we have a consumer mindset. We admit that we want personal peace and prosperity ahead of God's agenda. We admit that, for many of us, indifference and passivity characterize our lives. Remember our theme verse: *"The eyes of the Lord move to and fro throughout the [whole] earth that He may strongly support* [not weakly, not help you do a little better, but strongly support]*" you to do miraculous things* (see 2 Chronicles 16:9 NASB). What kind of people does He want to do that for? Those who are completely His.

Repentance means to have a change of mind. It means facing my indifference and selfishness with genuine sorrow and getting before God and doing what's right. That's what Nehemiah did! After he heard the bad news, he said, "Here's my life. I've got it made in the shade, but God's agenda is going down the tube." He wept. He fasted. He mourned. Try Nehemiah's approach. It may be deeply painful, but it will ultimately be powerfully freeing. To have your heart beat after God's heart and His agenda will bring new vitality and life and power as you have never experienced it.

You see, this second and most difficult step in developing a dislocated heart forces us to get our eyes off ourselves and on to God, to get our eyes off our own agendas and on to the needs and concerns of others. Be very careful as you move through this process. It is not a step to be taken lightly or quickly. But I am convinced that we can't develop dislocated hearts without it.

### 3. Thoughtful Consideration

A dislocated heart may display emotion, but a dislocated heart is not primarily an emotional response. A dislocated heart is honest about emotions and approaches life with thoughtful consideration. Given everything we've said in this chapter, *fear* is the primary emotion I find in others and myself, when we think seriously about allowing God to dislocate our hearts. We need to take these fears seriously. We need also to remember that God is mindful of our fear, and that it is fear that holds us back. As we begin taking steps toward a dislocated heart, these are some of the common fears we will wrestle with:

- What if God asks me to do something in the financial arena that could be especially challenging?
- What if God asks me to do something I don't really want to do?
- What if God asks me to go somewhere unfamiliar?
- What if God overwhelms me with the needs of the world?

If those thoughts are running through your mind, you're probably in good company. Fears are normal. God understands our fears. But we cannot let our fears hold us back from doing the will of God. In fact, I remember an intense prayer time with the elders of our church when the truth of this concept had a huge impact on us. We had clearly identified an area of need, and yet we knew that if we moved as an elder board to meet it, we might jeopardize the entire future of our church. The implications were staggering for all of us on the board and for the extended church body.

> I was almost too afraid to pray because the scope of the vision overwhelmed me. Then I heard the elder next to me humbly pray, "O God, I'm shaking in my boots."

Late one night, after lengthy discussions and a reaffirmation that we wanted to make decisions with dislocated hearts and had decided to move ahead under God's direction, we had a closing prayer time. I will never forget it. I was almost too afraid to pray because the scope of the vision overwhelmed me. Then I heard the elder next to me humbly pray, "O God, I'm shaking in my boots. If You would so be pleased, do what You choose to do with this church, whatever it is You want to do, but I'm afraid of what it might mean." I knew I wasn't alone in my fears.

Trusting God doesn't come easy to us. That's why it's called trust. It goes against our natural inclinations. Not long after that honest prayer, that elder sold his business so that he could leverage the fourth quarter of life for ministry. He deliberately turned his back on his safety net—retirement—and sold out to invest more time in other people for the kingdom of God. He became a Prime Mover for God's glory.

Carefully consider what a dislocated heart will involve. Don't go into any of this lightly. Don't simply get emotionally charged up. Don't think this is a shallow discipleship pep rally. Carefully consider what God may have you do.

### 4. Asking God for a Dislocated Heart

The fourth and unavoidable step in developing a dislocated heart is to ask God for one. Early in my walk with Christ I expressed my own fearful prayer, "God, I know that this is Your will. I know that You want me to have a dislocated heart, but I don't have one. I want to care more deeply and not live in fear, but that's not where I am right now." Then the Spirit of God prompted me, "Just ask Me for one. I'm good. I love you. I'm going to lead you in a way that will bring great delight and great reward. I'm good and I'm sovereign. I'm compassionate."

Then I thought, *Oh, yeah, I forgot about that. I was just feeling all of this demand and internal pressure.* I bowed my head and said, "God, I'm not sure what a dislocated heart looks like. But I'd like one. Would You give me one? If it takes time, it takes time. If it comes in degrees or all at once that's fine, but I want that."

I invite you to make that your prayer. In fact, why not set this book down for a few minutes and ponder where you are in your life with Christ? God has created you as His workmanship and wants to use your life beyond your wildest dreams (Ephesians 2:10). Every chapter in the adventure of holy ambition begins with a dislocated heart. Do you have one? Do you want one? Then carefully think through the four steps in developing a dislocated heart. Approach them as questions:

- Have I honestly *evaluated my own heart* and life?
- Have I *genuinely repented* of my consumer mind-set?
- Have I *carefully considered the implications* and dealt with my fears?
- Have I *asked God* for a dislocated heart?

Before we go to the next chapter, let me remind you that the danger in calling these "conditions for developing holy ambition," or even "phases in developing holy ambition," is the idea that once we've developed a dislocated heart we have stepped past a point in the journey and will move on. That is not the case. A dislocated heart travels with you. It must be maintained. It requires ongoing development. As you will discover by the end of our journey, if you don't already know it, all of the most important lessons in life require frequently repeated visits. I appreciate your company on the journey.

## TALK IT OVER

**Question from Chip on the video:** *On a scale of 1 to10 (1 = not at all and 10 = totally) give us a number that would indicate where you are in having a dislocated heart. Then, share briefly about why you gave yourself that rating.*

**1.** What are some of the top needs in your local community?

**2.** Are the needs around you on your spiritual radar? How soft is your heart toward people who are suffering?

**3.** The first step in developing a dislocated heart is honest, personal self-evaluation. Take a few moments and honestly share the condition of your heart toward people in need. Is it distracted? Hard? Soft and caring? Preoccupied? Engaged? Desensitized?

**4.** Another step that Chip mentioned in developing a dislocated heart is that of Thoughtful Consideration. If you were to really have a dislocated heart and get involved with some need that God lays on your heart, what would have to change in your life? What are some of the potential costs/sacrifices?

**5.** What causes you to have a "dislocated heart"? Is there some need that has captured your heart and is stirring you to action?

**6.** What does it look like for you to get out of your comfort zone?

Chip said "stepping outside the comfortable often begins with something very, very small . . . remember that even the largest task for God starts with a small step" (page 40).

What is one small step you could take this week to engage the needs around you?

**7.** Spend the last few minutes of your time together praying together. It can just be sentence prayers, but ask God to give you a dislocated heart.

## LIVE IT OUT

**1.** Take a walk around your neighborhood. See your neighborhood with spiritual eyes. Watch the news with an open heart to hear the voice of God.

**2.** Chip said, "God never does something great *through* us until He does something significant *in* us!" Consider following Nehemiah's example and set aside a time to fast and pray. Take the challenge of doing a twenty-four-hour fast as a group. Take the time you would normally spend eating and spend it in prayer. You might even want to gather as a group over lunchtime to pray together.

*"For the eyes of the Lord move to and fro throughout the earth that He may strongly support those whose heart is completely His."*

—2 CHRONICLES 16:9 NASB

# a broken
# SPIRIT

the second condition in developing holy ambition

---

Angie Thompson has a dislocated heart. When I hear her story, I find that Nehemiah's attitude fits right into the twenty-first century. She is part of an unbroken line of people throughout history whom God has used to demonstrate that His promises are true and dependable. When the newspaper headlines and talk radio's nonstop discussions threaten to depress us, we need flesh and blood examples like Nehemiah and Angie to remind us that God is still in control. God still has people who are daily making a difference for Him. It remains true that "the eyes of the Lord move to and fro throughout the earth that He may strongly support those whose heart is completely His" (2 Chronicles 16:9 NASB).

Some years ago, Angie Thompson took a trip to Romania. She was in her twenties, had recently graduated from college, and had landed an excellent job in Silicon Valley earning dream wages. But that short-term mission trip changed her life and countless others for all eternity.

In Romania she saw thousands of kids living on the streets, taking shelter in sewers, dying of hunger, disease, and neglect. Something deep inside Angie Thompson changed. She reached a point where she could no longer stand what she was seeing. But instead of turning away from those children living as animals, she moved toward them. She decided that although she was only one person, she had to do something. In her own words, "I just couldn't see myself going back to my secure, comfortable world, sipping lattes at lunch, knowing that those kids were living in such deplorable conditions."

Angie is an ordinary woman with ordinary contacts and ordinary talents. But she doesn't have an ordinary vision. And she serves an extraordinary God. Those are sure signs of a dislocated heart.

Eventually, Angie's response became a place: a shelter called City of Hope. Growing from seeds planted by one woman with a passion, this ministry feeds children, gets them off the streets, turns their lives around, and offers them hope for the future. Our church, following her lead, has sent scores of people, donated hundreds of thousands of dollars, and built an orphanage in cooperation with Assist International and the City of Hope.

For many on our teams, those trips are life changing. Their hearts get dislocated. They return with a new understanding of what God can do with a single life that belongs completely to Him. Over fifteen hundred people helped finance our most recent project, personally represented on-site by eighty workers who traveled to Romania. Why? Because one young woman refused to allow the status quo to determine her life. She had a dislocated heart.

The enemy of your soul uses at least three weapons to prevent or neutralize a dislocated heart: discouragement, disillusionment, and desensitization. I think the last one is the one he uses most effectively in our culture. We are jaded and desensitized to horrific events and escalating evil. Atrocities, tragedies, and disasters move us—for a little while. The news media feed us a steady diet of sensational stories, each designed not to move us to action but to keep us watching. Success is measured not by the changes brought about by their stories but by the size of the market share they keep glued to the monitors.

Neither discouragement nor disillusionment needs to be employed by Satan because we don't usually get that far. Desensitization quickly takes over. Last week's exposé or tragic story is old news. Feelings of compassion or concern that were stirred up over those events cannot be spared any longer. They are needed for the new breaking stories. In the process, our hearts get twisted, pulled, and punched but never quite stay dislocated.

So what does it take to prevent a dislocated heart from becoming desensitized? What happened in Angie Thomson and the scores who have followed her example and who kept the flames of concern burning when they returned home? The answer may surprise you. Our compassion and concern must drive us back to a fresh view of God, a clear view of ourselves, and a new view of others. That, in turn, will bring us to the second condition required to have a life that makes a difference for God: *a broken spirit*.

> **There is something God hates 100 percent of the time.**

## GOD REJECTS PRIDE

Before we focus on the next critical phase God takes every believer through whom He uses greatly, we must first lay the groundwork by thinking for a few moments about our present view of God. We need to get a clear view of God Himself. For until we grasp some crucial aspects of the way God has revealed Himself, we will not be able to grasp the second condition of holy ambition God is looking for in our lives.

God has stated categorically that He hates one thing 100 percent of the time. God has always hated this character trait and has declared that He will always hate it. God abhors this trait in both individuals and groups. When the Old Testament prophets spoke on God's behalf, they often condemned entire nations because their attitude as a people demonstrated this characteristic. God condemned some of His angels for this trait. Do you know that one thing that God absolutely hates? God hates pride.

The Scriptures are unmistakably clear on this point. Proverbs 8:13 says, "To fear the Lord is to hate evil; I hate pride and arrogance, evil behavior and perverse speech." James 4:6 tells us, "God opposes the proud but gives grace to the humble." In other words, as the Lord's eyes go to and fro across the earth,

He responds in a certain, predictable, and emphatic way when He finds a prideful heart. God opposes or resists that heart. God is opposed to the proud 100 percent of the time.

What is pride? Pride is rooted in self-dependency and self-focus. Pride can be strutting our stuff: "I don't need God. I can do this on my own." Or pride can be disguised as humility: "I'm nothing. I'm nobody. God could never use me." Both of these extremes share a common feature: the focus is on us. God hates it. There is only one center of the universe worthy of all our attention, and that center is God. If we make ourselves the center of our universe, we are engaging in what the Bible calls pride and arrogance. This attitude is neither a minor glitch nor something God merely dislikes. It is not something He overlooks. He loathes pride.

## GOD LOVES AND RESPONDS TO A BROKEN SPIRIT

Yet God has also revealed what He appreciates, loves, and always responds to with favor. He finds this character trait in people who are otherwise very different from one another. The backgrounds of the people who possess this quality can be placed everywhere on the continuum from morally pure lives to lives marred by prostitution, drugs, perversions, and crimes. When God finds this quality, God responds—not sometimes, not maybe, but *always*. No matter what the pedigree or baggage, God pours out grace and love 100 percent of the time when He sees this quality in our hearts and minds.

Do you know what that character trait is? A broken spirit. We have God's Word on it. David wrote one of the classic passages of Scripture about this side of God. This was the man God had previously described as a "man after his [God's] own heart" (1 Samuel 13:14). Yet David coveted another man's wife, committed adultery, betrayed and murdered the husband, lied to God's prophet, and broke all Ten Commandments.

Then God confronted him with his sin.

In Psalm 51 we have a prayer that records David's return to God. In this prayer, David stated some very interesting things about what it means to establish right standing with God. Verse 16 says, "You do not delight in sacrifice, or I would bring it; you do not take pleasure in burnt offerings." David understood that God is not impressed, appeased, or fooled by external actions.

In other words, David told God, "You know where I've been; you know what I've done. I'm ashamed. I feel as badly as anyone could." The writer of so many of the psalms continued to express his realization that calves, burnt offerings, religious duties, or money—none of this—would be acceptable to God. He went on. *"The sacrifices of God are a broken spirit; a broken and contrite heart, O God, you will not despise"* (Psalm 51:17). In other words, no matter what we have been or what we have done, God will always welcome and embrace us when we come to Him with a broken spirit.

## A CONTRITE AND LOWLY SPIRIT

When people first start thinking about a broken spirit, they often ask, "Is this just feeling bad about myself?" No. "Is this just groveling in the dirt?" No. "Should we get our noses on the carpet and feel like we are terrible people?" No. "Is it tears?" Not necessarily. What, then, is a broken spirit? A broken spirit is an attitude of desperate dependency and humility that allows us to come to God fully expecting that He will say, "I greet you; I love you; I'll lift you up; I'll use you." The original language behind the expression *broken spirit* is fascinating. In Hebrew, the term indicates an experience of being "crushed" or "bruised."

The word itself is used only four times in the Old Testament, and it consistently describes spiritual responses. A broken spirit or heart is associated with a contrite heart. The contrite spirit or heart describes an attitude of humility. The two characteristics (brokenness and humility) appear together in a person's life. The first has to do with what has been removed or demoted from a central place in a person's life. The second has to do with a genuine self-effacing attitude. To put it another way, a broken spirit had to do with an absolute sense of dependency on and total need for God. And as it turns out, no matter what the starting point, these character traits appear most clearly in lives that have hit bottom. Such people often discover more about God than those who appear morally upright but have never really met God.

I find that people, including me, need to be reminded to read the New Testament with our "church glasses" off. We confuse familiarity with understanding. But when we let the Scriptures speak for themselves, we find many passages that don't seem to make sense. You don't have to read far in the Gospels to note the following pattern. Jesus, though He is God the Son, living in this world to reveal the Father, acted in unexpected ways. He stiff-armed and offended very religious people. He appeared unimpressed by those who knew the Bible and kept all the rules. He was merciless with self-righteousness. People who looked down their noses on others got their noses out of joint when Jesus passed by.

> *If the idea of walking with Jesus doesn't make you uncomfortable, you haven't thought seriously enough about His presence in your life.*

Remember Jesus' visit to the home of a Pharisee? A woman approached as He reclined at the table, and she wept over His feet. She dried them with her hair. Her humility and vulnerability were undeniable, but so was the fact that she had broken every cultural norm of the day. Those watching were stunned by her behavior and shocked at Jesus' failure to reject her. They saw this as clear indication that Jesus didn't understand or know the woman's reputation and therefore must not be who He claimed to be.

But Jesus turned the tables on them with an indictment of their own failures. They had been grossly negligent in even the common courtesies extended to a guest. Their painstaking attention to so much as a sliver of inappropriate behavior on Jesus' part had left them vulnerable to a blindness-inducing log in their own eyes. They couldn't see past the woman's failures to their own desperate needs. Jesus recognized and deeply appreciated the woman's gesture. He knew her life.

Jesus' comments to the Pharisee and his friends might be summarized this way. "Friend, you have no idea what just happened here. I arrived as a guest in your home and you did nothing to make Me feel welcome. You are ignorant of your own need. You think that you are right with God because you have figured out how to keep a carefully edited moral list. She walked in from a shattered life without any pretense of righteousness. The difference between her and you is that she has a broken spirit. She came desperate, spiritually bankrupt, and expressed her sorrow and brokenness. The only need you see is the need to condemn her. She's going to walk away forgiven and clean. You'll walk away justifying yourself in vain."

If the idea of walking with Jesus doesn't make you uncomfortable, you haven't thought seriously enough about His presence in your life. The passed-down, packaged Jesus turns out to be quite different than the One who steps alive and kicking from the pages of Scripture. Jesus broke many rules established by people because He saw that their purpose was to nullify God's rules for living. A life or a church that is going to be an effective tool in Jesus' plans will take unexpected shapes and do unexpected things. It will break molds. It will change what people think is important and hold fiercely to what others are treating as minor priorities. Such a life and such a church will be characterized by *a dislocated heart* and *a broken spirit*.

God has told us His desires. We don't have to guess about His priorities. Note these words from Isaiah: "For this is what the high and lofty One says—he who lives forever, whose name is holy: 'I live in a high and holy place, but also with him who is contrite and lowly in spirit, to revive the spirit of the lowly and to revive the heart of the contrite'" (Isaiah 57:15). I challenge you to carefully meditate on this passage. As you do, you will discover the only two places where God dwells completely unhindered. The God of the universe dwells in a high and lofty place—the center of the universe. And where else? With those who are "contrite and lowly in spirit."

> *Those are the only two places where there is enough room for God to be all that He really is.*

Those are the only two places where there is enough room for God to be all that He really is. Whenever God is recognized for who He really is, He will manifest His power and His presence in ways that transform lives and shatter the status quo. God has provided His clear profile in Scripture. A preoccupation with ourselves, our agenda, and our preconceived ideas, and a motivation to achieve personal peace and prosperity (i.e., pride) will be met with resistance from our heavenly Father. By contrast, a genuine sense of desperation and dependency on Him and Him alone (i.e., a broken spirit) will be met with grace, power, and supernatural provision.

If you are like me, you long to have a broken spirit but are well aware that pride in its many insidious forms has a significant hold on your heart. So how does it work? How can we develop this "broken spirit" that God promises to respond to 100 percent of the time?

## THREE KEYS TO DEVELOPING A BROKEN SPIRIT

The answer to this question is found in Nehemiah 1:4–11. In this passage we eavesdrop on one of Nehemiah's most powerful and revealing prayers. Before we look at the parts of the prayer, I invite you to read the entire outpouring of Nehemiah's heart:

> When I heard these things, I sat down and wept. For some days I mourned and fasted and prayed before the God of heaven. Then I said:
>
> "O Lord, God of heaven, the great and awesome God, who keeps his covenant of love with those who love him and obey his commands, let your ear be attentive and your eyes open to hear the prayer your servant is praying before you day and night for your servants, the people of Israel. I confess the sins we Israelites, including myself and my father's house, have committed against you. We have acted very wickedly toward you. We have not obeyed the commands, decrees and laws you gave your servant Moses.
> "Remember the instruction you gave your servant Moses, saying, 'If you are unfaithful, I will scatter you among the nations, but if you return to me and obey my commands, then even if your exiled people are at the farthest horizon, I will gather them from there and bring them to the place I have chosen as a dwelling for my Name.'
> "They are your servants and your people, whom you redeemed by your great strength and your mighty hand. O Lord, let your ear be attentive to the prayer of this your servant and to the prayer of your servants who delight in revering your name. Give your servant success today by granting him favor in the presence of this man."
>
> NEHEMIAH 1:4–11

### *A High View of God*

The first key is this: A broken spirit begins with a restored view of God. It's seeing God afresh. A dislocated heart is created by an ever-expanding view of the needs of the world from God's perspective. A broken spirit begins when we look up from the needs of the creation to see the Creator. A dislocated heart is overwhelmed by a problem or need; a broken spirit is overwhelmed by God. We won't see the possibility of solution for the needs of the world unless we see that God is large enough to meet those needs. Not a scaled-down, human version of almighty God, but the awesome, humbling, overwhelming Creator behind the universe.

Read again Nehemiah 1:4–5:

When I heard these words [the bad news about Jerusalem: the discouraged people; the wall being torn down; the gates burned with fire; the people in disgrace], I sat down and wept and mourned for days [we learned that he wept and grieved for about four months]; and I was fasting and praying before the God of heaven. [Now listen to his prayer] I said, "I beseech You, O Lord [Yahweh, God's personal name; His covenant name] God of heaven [He's all-powerful], the great and awesome God."

NEHEMIAH 1:4–5 NASB

Nehemiah was approaching God from a foreign and isolated land. He had been under the influence of the Babylonians. They had a god on every corner. Astrology and all its spin-off ideas originated there. Yet Nehemiah's view of God contained the majesty and holiness of God. The phrase "God of heaven, the great and awesome God" includes the idea that God is holy, totally all-powerful. God is the biggest version of what we can conceive. Instead, we are made in God's image, which means that we are hints of all that God is in fact.

Nehemiah's prayer continues:

"Who preserves the covenant and lovingkindness for those who love Him [God is compassionate, tender, understanding] and keep His commandments, let Your ear now be attentive and Your eyes open to hear the prayer of Your servant which I am praying before You now, day and night [not on a whim; this is extended, in-depth time], on behalf of the sons of Israel Your servants."

NEHEMIAH 1:5–6 NASB

Nehemiah begins his prayer with a high view of God. He knows God's personal name. In fact, this passage, verses 4–11, includes forty-four references to God by either personal pronoun, name, or reference. Don't forget this: Nehemiah prayed God-centered prayers. I don't mean to be critical, but listen to our typical prayers. We pray people-centered prayers. We pray circumstance-centered prayers. We pray God-fix-this-for-me, God-fix-that-for-me kind of prayers. "God, make this happen." "God, do that." "God, make me happy." "God, help us have a good time." These kind of prayers indicate that we are taking ourselves all too seriously and not taking God very seriously at all!

A broken spirit begins with a high view of God. He is Yahweh; I Am That I Am; the Ever-existing One. Above everything, a broken spirit knows the God of heaven. He is great. He is powerful. *He is holy.* He is loving.

In Isaiah 6, we get another picture of a man who had a high view of God. It says:

> In the year that King Uzziah died, I saw the Lord seated on a throne,
> high and exalted, and the train of his robe filled the temple. Above him were seraphs,
> each with six wings: With two wings they covered their faces, with two they covered
> their feet, and with two they were flying. And they were calling to one another:

> "Holy, holy, holy is the Lord Almighty;
> the whole earth is full of his glory."

> At the sound of their voices the doorposts and thresholds shook and the
> temple was filled with smoke.
>
> ISAIAH 6:1–4

Isaiah's response is not one we hear much in our day. "'Woe to me! . . . I am ruined! For I am a man of unclean lips, and I live among a people of unclean lips, and my eyes have seen the King, the Lord Almighty'" (Isaiah 6:5).

When was the last time you were alone with God and saw so clearly who He was that you started to see more clearly who you really were? Contrary to much popular teaching in our day, God isn't just our good buddy. He's not the genie in the bottle or a security blanket. He's not the latest self-help guru. He is holy. Life is not about getting Him to fulfill our agenda; it's about His agenda being fulfilled on this earth. And amazingly, He will let us get in on it if we choose to obey.

Notice what happens next:

> Then one of the seraphs flew to me with a live coal in his hand, which he
> had taken with tongs from the altar. With it he touched my mouth and said,
> "See, this has touched your lips; your guilt is taken away and your sin atoned for."
> Then I heard the voice of the Lord saying, "Whom shall I send?
> And who will go for us?"
> And I said, "Here am I. Send me!"
> ISAIAH 6:6–8

Do you see the picture? Isaiah has a broken spirit. A broken spirit begins with a high view of God, a holy view of God. Then, a broken spirit leads us to an accurate view of ourselves. After that, a renewed commitment to God's agenda will follow. In *The Knowledge of the Holy* ([New York: Harper & Row, 1961; Jubilee ed., 1975], 9), A.W. Tozer wrote:

> What comes into our minds when we think about God is the most impor-
> tant thing about us. The history of mankind will probably show that no people
> have ever risen above its religion, and man's spiritual history will positively
> demonstrate that no religion has ever been greater than its idea of God. Wor-
> ship is pure or base. The worshiper attains a high or a low thought of God. For
> this reason, the gravest question before the church is always, God himself.
> The most portentous fact about anyone is not what he is doing at a given time,
> what he may say or do, but what in his deep heart he conceives God to be like.

What is your view of God? Are your prayers God-centered prayers? A bro-ken spirit begins in the presence of God. When you see God for who He is, it gets very easy to have a broken spirit. So how is your prayer life? What comes to your mind when you bow your head to pray? Do you have a high and lofty view of God, or has He unconsciously become your self-help genie, your good buddy, your back-up plan when all else fails? We will never have a broken spirit unless we have a high and lofty view of God. And as we have seen from Isaiah and Nehemiah, a high and lofty view of God is a prerequisite and allows us a clearer view of ourselves.

## AN ACCURATE VIEW OF OURSELVES

The first key led Nehemiah, as it will lead us, to the second one: an accurate view of himself. He says,

> "I confess the sins we Israelites, including myself and my father's house, have committed against you. We have acted very wickedly toward you. [Then he gets specific. He doesn't stick with anything in general. "You know, we had a couple of bad days."] We have not obeyed the commands, decrees and laws you gave your servant Moses."
>
> NEHEMIAH 1:6–7

An accurate view of ourselves will always lead to confession, down deep in our hearts. It was true for Nehemiah. It was true for Isaiah. And it is true for you and me. When I get really close to God, what I find is that I'm not doing anywhere near as well as I thought I was doing. I find motives in me that are just so ugly, so arrogant. When I draw near to God and I have special times with Him and see who He really is, I realize that I'm about as indispensable as mud. Your life and my life are just like a wink. The world was going on before we came, and it's going to be zooming on after we leave.

*Repentance happens sometimes in big installments and sometimes in little installments throughout the day.*

That doesn't mean that we are insignificant. In fact, God says that you and I are valuable and loved. But when we get an accurate view of ourselves we must do the hard work that is so uncommon in our day. We must repent. This happens sometimes in big installments and sometimes in little installments throughout the day. If you're a little foggy on what repentance is all about, read James 4. He tells us exactly how to do it.

> Submit yourselves, then, to God. Resist the devil, and he will flee from you.
> Come near to God [look at this promise] and he will come near to you.
> Wash your hands, you sinners [if your hands are involved in things that are wrong,
> wash them; cleanse them], and purify your hearts, you double-minded. Grieve
> [let it get down under your skin; let it get into your heart; get real, get honest],
> mourn and wail. Change your laughter to mourning and your joy to gloom.
> Humble yourselves before the Lord, and he will lift you up.
>
> JAMES 4:7–10

The goal of a broken spirit isn't to feel terrible about ourselves. It's just to be accurate, to grasp a fresh view and understand the moral and personal chasm between God and us. When we approach God that way, here's what He won't do. He won't push our faces down. He won't say, "Yeah, you *are* a terrible person." What He will say is, "I know all about you and about all your sin. That's why I sent My Son." God's grace always moves toward genuine brokenness.

Yet until we get a high view of God and an accurate view of ourselves, Jesus will never mean that much to us. Until we see the extent of our need, we can never appreciate the significance of our Savior. Jesus covers and bridges the distance between a holy God and sinful man. That's you and that's me. He died on the cross to pay for your sin and mine. He loves us. When we come even as believers with a broken spirit, He reminds us that He wants to lift us up. God says of our sins and failures, "You've owned them. You've confessed them. I will forgive you and cleanse you. I will set you up and I will use you, even you."

The New Testament is filled with what? Failures! Yeah, I love that. You know why? Because I'm one. It's filled with people who failed miserably, whose lives didn't work, who were spiritually bankrupt. They came to Jesus, and He cleansed and forgave them. We may think of the apostle Paul as a great hero, but before he came to Christ he was a murderer and persecutor of the church. You may think you're not qualified. Wrong! You *are* qualified. Christ makes you qualified to be used by God. A broken spirit, that deep sense of your need and dependency moves you in the right direction.

## A RENEWED COMMITMENT TO GOD'S AGENDA

First, a high view of God restores an accurate view of ourselves. Then, when we begin to see who God is and who we are, we experience God's cleansing and forgiveness through repentance. That brings us to the third key in developing a broken spirit. We realize (are you ready for this?) that life isn't about us. You know what that is called? Humility. A broken spirit *results in a renewed commitment to fulfill God's agenda instead of our own plans.* When we cooperate with God's agenda, He is so loving and so gracious that He also fulfills many of our desires too; a broken spirit will drastically refocus our priorities and our prayers,

Notice what Nehemiah did. He saw God. He confessed. Then he talked to God about God's own promises. He said, "Please remember what you told your servant Moses: 'If you are unfaithful to me, I will scatter you among the nations. But if you return to me and obey my commands and live by them, then even if you are exiled to the ends of the earth, I will bring you back to the place I have chosen for my name to be honored'" (Nehemiah 1:8–9 NLT).

Nehemiah prayed not only God-centered and gut-wrenchingly honest prayers but also promise-centered prayers. He quoted Deuteronomy 30:2–7 and alluded to Exodus 32:10–12. He said, "God, You made a promise about sending us to the ends of the earth if we turned away from You; but You also promised that if we turned from our sin, You would return us to Your holy land and restore us." Notice the request.

"They are Your servants and Your people whom You redeemed by Your great power
and by Your strong hand. O Lord, I beseech You, may Your ear be attentive to the
prayer of Your servant and the prayer of Your servants who delight to revere Your name,
and make Your servant successful today and grant him compassion before this man."
NEHEMIAH 1:10–11 NASB

Did you notice how many times Nehemiah talked to God about His plan, His servants, and His agenda? And do you know what he was saying to God? "You're the One who made the promises. I'm trusting You to keep them." A broken spirit leads to a commitment to God's agenda. Out of his months of grieving and praying, a personal role became clear to Nehemiah. "I'm going to go and talk to the king," he prayed. "It may cost me my life, but I'm interceding first with my mouth, and I'm coming to You with a broken spirit that I know You will in no way cast out." When Nehemiah said, "I'm going to follow this up with a radical step of faith where I trust You to show up," he had entered the next phase of holy ambition, which we will discuss in the next chapter.

## YOUR HEART

So often in our day, instead of having a big God, we have big problems. So often in our day, we feel like things are impossible and we forget that Nehemiah prayed this prayer in the midst of a culture strikingly like ours. His was a pluralistic, god-on-every-corner world—just like ours. Left to ourselves, we tend to talk about how bad everything is as though God were distant, uninvolved, and has maybe even lost control of His creation. Actually, Nehemiah's situation was as bad as ours, if not worse. But when God, in that day, went looking for a man or woman who would stand in the gap for Him, someone He could strongly support, He found Nehemiah. God identified Nehemiah's dislocated heart and readiness to develop a broken spirit.

That broken spirit grew in Nehemiah as it can grow in us. First, by spending time in the presence of God until we see Him for who He really is. Second, by developing an accurate view of ourselves, with the repentance that must follow. Only then are we reinvigorated, not in our own strength, but based on God's promises about what He is going to do. That truth of the matter is that life really is about God, and He is going to fulfill His agenda. He is simply looking for a few good men and women who will take Him seriously, who will be so fully devoted, with all their hearts, that He can strongly support them.

To what degree do you have a broken spirit? It's a process, isn't it? But it starts in a moment of time. Do you want to have an impact? Do you want to be a person whom the eyes of the Lord see and whom He strongly supports?

You must let God work deeply. He must work *in* you before He will work significantly *through* you. Until you make prayer a priority, progress and power will never be a reality. *Prayer is the assembly line for a broken spirit, where we broaden and deepen our understanding of God; where we sharpen our under-*

*standing of ourselves; where we renew our deep commitment to God's agenda.*

I don't mean superficial, rote prayers. I don't mean just practicing-the-presence-of-God prayers. I don't mean catching-God-on-the-run prayers. I'm talking about the kind of prayers that are God-centered. They take time. They are promise-focused. They are gut-wrenchingly honest. They are moments like this one, when you recognize the Spirit of God calling out to you and whispering, "You're the one. I am looking for you. I have a place of service in My plans that fits exactly how I made you. Do you know Me well enough yet to trust Me?"

Consider answering the Spirit's question with a time of unhurried prayer before you go to the next chapter. Why not think of the things and people that matter most to you and pray some specific promises from God's Word over their lives?

## TALK IT OVER

**Question from Chip on the video:** *If God really wants to work in us before He works through us, where do you think He wants to work in you? Complete the following statement: I think God wants to work in . . .*

**1.** The needs around us are often overwhelming. Each day the headlines are filled with stories of human tragedy and injustice. So, how do you keep your heart soft toward the needs around you and not let your heart become cynical and desensitized?

**2.** Read Psalm 51:10–17. David wrote these words in response to being confronted about his adulterous relationship with Bathsheba. What can we learn about having a "broken spirit" from these verses?

**3.** Chip mentioned a story from Luke 7:36–48. Have someone read the story. What evidence is there that the Pharisees didn't have a broken spirit? And, what evidence is there that this woman had a broken spirit?

**4.** Read Nehemiah's prayer (Nehemiah 1:4–11). What stands out to you in this prayer? How is Nehemiah's prayer different from those we often hear today?

**5.** Chip said, "If the idea of walking with Jesus doesn't make you uncomfortable, you haven't thought seriously enough about His presence in your life" (page 56–57). What about following Jesus has made you uncomfortable?

**6.** Read James 4:7–10. Why is this passage so important to having a holy ambition? What part of the passage do you most need to apply?

## LIVE IT OUT

**1.** Read Psalm 51 every day this week. Spend time really soaking in the "broken spirit" of David and letting God speak to you about your own brokenness.

**2.** Set aside an hour in this coming week just to be alone with God. Pray "God-centered" prayers and allow time for God to speak to you.

*"For the eyes of the Lord move to and fro throughout the earth that He may strongly support those whose heart is completely His."*

—2 Chronicles 16:9 NASB

# a radical
# FAITH

the third condition in developing holy ambition

You can learn what it takes to make a difference for God in practically no time at all. This entire book will only take you a few hours to read. Many others have written about these principles. You can discover and study them on your own in God's Word.

But *learning* what it takes and actually *making a difference* for God each require a different pace. You can sprint to the knowing, but the doing is a marathon. Reading about a dislocated heart won't necessarily give you one. Browsing a chapter on a broken spirit may leave yours intact. But the closing thought in that last chapter reminded you that these matters ultimately boil down to God's work in your life and your willingness to participate in that work. What we are seeing in Nehemiah's life is that God does much of that foundational preparation in the context of prayer.

Up to this point, most of the work involved in experiencing a dislocated heart and developing a broken spirit has been internal, or private. Cultivating a dislocated heart and a broken spirit occur in the soil of a deepening prayer life. Others may or may not be aware of the changes that God is bringing about in you as your heart is dislocated and your spirit broken. Those closest to you may comment that something seems to be happening to you. But they will definitely witness the next phase of a growing holy ambition as you begin to practice a radical faith. Radical faith still includes a lot of internal work, but it has an unavoidable external aspect. Dislocation and brokenness may well be private matters; radical faith is public. Dislocation and brokenness develop behind the scenes; radical faith puts you right out there on stage.

> **People seem much more concerned about the right to choose than choosing what is right.**

## THE PUBLIC ARENA

Have you noticed the tendency in our culture to keep a distance between "faith" and "public"? You and I know we live in a pluralistic society. Part of what that means officially is that we can speak boldly about everyone's right to believe whatever they choose to believe. But we're not supposed to speak about what we have actually chosen to believe. Apparently we're all for letting people choose, but not so sure that people should be clearly informed about the implications of their choices.

The underlying and seldom stated idea seems to be that the specific choices don't really matter, only that people make them. People seem much more concerned about the right to choose than choosing what is right. The apostle Paul was speaking directly to Christians today when he wrote, "How, then, can they call on the one they have not believed in? And how can they believe in the one of whom they have not heard? And how can they hear without someone preaching to them?" (Romans 10:14).

The public arena is a loud place. When it comes to making their faith public, most Christians feel like someone who has been in a soundproof booth stepping suddenly onto a stadium field in the middle of an exciting football game. The noise is deafening and the action confusing. The details are discouraging and overwhelming. I don't need to go through the list of what we notice in our culture that stands in blatant and direct opposition to God's wishes. As soon as we attempt to understand our surroundings, we tend to get either very angry or very discouraged. The shift in ethics and morality in just my lifetime shocks me when I ponder it.

## PERSPECTIVE

When I'm left to myself, I'm tempted to think the times are worse than ever and that life is terrible. What's the use in speaking when no one wants to listen? Then, when I open my Bible and look at history, I realize that the world we are living in is far from being the worst it has ever been. God's people have actually experienced much greater difficulties in the past than we do today. Christians today, particularly in Western nations, are in more danger of being entertained and bored into oblivion than of being persecuted. We enjoy amazing freedoms that far too often we are squandering.

But there have indeed been desperate moments for believers in the past. There were times when the entire nation of Israel was close to being annihilated. God chose a convicted and shamed murderer named Moses to lead to freedom a people crushed by slavery. When Israel faced a holocaust in Persia, a young woman in her early twenties named Esther risked her life when she said, "I'll go before the king."

There have been periods of immense moral decline throughout biblical, church, and world history. Imagine how bad things were during the time of Ezekiel. The people of Israel, God's people, were worshiping idols such as Moloch and sacrificing their children in the fire to appease the gods. God spoke through the prophet Ezekiel. Chapter 22 of the book of Ezekiel outlines the desperate evil in society. For twenty-nine verses God describes the way His people have wandered from Him. His indictment is devastating. The people face multiple counts of blatant sin yet seem oblivious to their danger. The outlook appears hopeless.

Then, in verse 30, God says something I believe is just as true today as it was then: "*I searched for a man among them who would build up the wall and stand in the gap before Me for the land, so that I would not destroy it*" (Ezekiel 22:30 NASB). As our theme verse states, "The eyes of the Lord move to and fro throughout the earth" (2 Chronicles 16:9 NASB). God was looking. Yet Ezekiel 22:30 closes with one of the saddest phrases in all of Scripture. God says, "*But I found no one*" (NASB). How tragic it would be if, after looking at your life and mine, God reported the same disappointment in His quest for a life with holy ambition: "But I found no one."

During times of peril and moral decline God is always searching for a man; God is searching for a woman; God is searching for a student who will build up the wall and stand in the gap. Someone who will have a radical faith and say, "You know, the world may be collapsing around me, but in my little sphere, I'm going to make a difference. I'm going to step out; I'm going to have a radical faith." I'm convinced that the person who says that and then follows up with action demonstrates that he or she already has a dislocated heart and a broken spirit that results in a radical faith.

## NEHEMIAH'S RADICAL FAITH

Our model for radical faith is Nehemiah. Let's see how God used one man to change the history of his world. We pick up the events at the end of the first chapter of the book of Nehemiah. "O Lord," Nehemiah prays, "let your ear be attentive to the prayer of this your servant and to the prayer of your servants who delight in revering your name. Give your servant success today by granting him favor in the presence of this man" (Nehemiah 1:11). Then he adds, as an explanatory note for the reader, "I was cupbearer to the king" (v. 11).

As we've seen before, the Bible captures volumes in a single sentence. Much like the biblical queen Esther, Nehemiah realized that the place where God had placed him indicated a certain responsibility. At a time of crisis for the Jewish people, Mordecai, Queen Esther's uncle, told her:

> "Do not think that because you are in the king's house you alone of all the
> Jews will escape. For if you remain silent at this time, relief and deliverance for
> the Jews will arise from another place, but you and your father's family will perish.

And who knows but that you have come to royal position for such a time as this?"

ESTHER 4:13–14

When Nehemiah asked God for favor before the king, he was stepping out in a radical faith that gave God lots of room to operate. Nehemiah wasn't sure what God would do, but he made clear that he was enlisting in the plan. Four months had passed since the heartbreaking news had reached Nehemiah that Jerusalem was still in ruins.

The second chapter of Nehemiah begins with a glimpse of life in the throne room.

> In the month of Nisan in the twentieth year of King Artaxerxes, when wine
> was brought for him, I took the wine and gave it to the king. I had not been sad in
> his presence before; so the king asked me, "Why does your face look so sad
> when you are not ill? This can be nothing but sadness of heart."
> I was very much afraid.
>
> NEHEMIAH 2:1–2

Nehemiah had good reason to be afraid. He was one royal frown away from having a very bad day. Why? It was the goal of every person, especially the wine taster, to make the king a happy camper. It was a ruthless time in history. On a whim, people were executed. A king's disinterest or displeasure often meant instant death for anyone who dared to complicate the king's life.

I love the statement, "I was very much afraid." I know the feeling. Do you? If you take the challenge of radical faith, you are going to be afraid. I guarantee it. *I'm afraid.* Yet it's okay to be afraid. When God asks you to do something you haven't done before—even something out of character for you—it will stretch your talent and your finances and your time. It will expose your insecurities. You *should* be afraid.

But whereas fear usually causes us to reconsider our commitments, the fear that comes with radical faith simply keeps very clear in our minds who is in charge. When we are afraid, we can come to God and tell Him so. God doesn't panic; neither should we. Notice what Nehemiah did about his fear.

He acted. *Radical faith doesn't mean that you are not afraid. Radical faith just means that you are willing to act despite your fears.*

So Nehemiah, fears and all, spoke up, "But I said to the king, 'May the king live forever! [Nehemiah knew it doesn't hurt to practice good protocol and PR.] Why should my face not look sad when the city where my fathers are buried lies in ruins, and its gates have been destroyed by fire?'" (Nehemiah 2:3).

> The quickie prayer was answered because it was part of a much longer, ongoing conversation between Nehemiah and God.

Notice that Nehemiah answered the question with a short, clear answer expressed as another question. He respectfully asked the king to step into his shoes (or heart) for a moment. At the same time, he also put himself at the disposal of the king. It might well have been the royal response to say, "It doesn't matter what happens close by or far away, Nehemiah. When you're in my house, I expect your face to look happy. Any more of these displays of emotion and you'll lose both your face and the head it's connected to."

Fortunately, Proverbs 21:1 was proved exactly true in this occasion: "The king's heart is in the hand of the Lord; he directs it like a watercourse wherever he pleases." The king cut through mounds of red tape when he answered Nehemiah's question with yet another question of his own: "What is it you want?" (Nehemiah 2:4). Talk about an open door!

This was one of those turning points in history that would be great to watch as an instant replay in heaven. What tone do you think the king used? Was he suspicious of Nehemiah's motives, or did he ask with a joyful, now-I-finally-get-to-do-something-for-you kind of smile? Nehemiah's next comment tells us that the outcome was still in doubt.

"Then I prayed to the God of heaven [one of those quick, "O God, help me!" prayers], and I answered the king, 'If it pleases the king and if your servant has found favor in his sight, let him send me to the city in Judah where my fathers are buried so that I can rebuild it'" (Nehemiah 2:4).

I'll bet that when Nehemiah's heart was dislocated by the news from Jerusalem, his first thought wasn't, *Well, I'll just ask the king for permission to go back and rebuild it myself.* It took four months to get to that point. Along the way his spirit was broken. How? He had to submit his life and his plan to God's will. Out of that brokenness came his willingness and preparation for the radical step of faith he just took.

Success wasn't guaranteed. God might have had the king come up with a different plan. Nehemiah simply asked the king for basic permission. The quickie prayer was answered because it was part of a much longer, ongoing conversation between Nehemiah and God. When you get to the point of taking a radical step of faith, you may find yourself in the very same position. You may have to ask someone important in your life—a spouse, a parent, a boss—for permission to do what God has dislocated your heart to do.

Nehemiah's request provoked yet another question, perhaps inspired by a look between the king and the queen. "Then the king, with the queen sitting beside him, asked me, 'How long will your journey take, and when will you get back?' It pleased the king to send me; so I set a time" (Nehemiah 2:6). The queen would have been concerned over how long her husband was going to be endangered by the cupbearer's absence. The fact that Nehemiah's timetable satisfied them is yet another clue that God was at work. God responded powerfully to Nehemiah's step of faith.

## WHAT IS RADICAL FAITH?

*Radical faith is choosing to step out to fulfill God's clearly defined will at possible great personal risk and sacrifice.* The situation will seldom be life and death, as it was in Nehemiah's case, but it will always be demanding. I would challenge you to casually read through your Bible and see if that isn't the pattern. Repeatedly, God seems to say, "My people are being destroyed; Moses, will you go? My people are going to be destroyed; Esther, will you go? The Gentiles need to know I'm their Savior, too; Paul, will you go?" You practice radical faith in those moments in which God's ownership of your life becomes the central reason for your actions. Radical faith is not a faith you simply *possess*; it's a faith you *practice*!

Faithful men and women in Scripture and throughout history have taken a step of great personal risk and sacrifice. What happens? God shows up.

Those people make a difference. God meets their radical faith with supernatural action!

## NOW WHAT?

I'm convinced that opinion polls are highly overrated and a very poor way to make decisions. Polls report the knee-jerk reactions of the masses, yet we use them to determine everything. The fact of the matter is, most of us are sheep. If someone says, "This is what is politically correct or spiritually correct," and someone champions the idea by saying, "This is where we're going," and they act as though they know what they're talking about, you know what happens? We follow them.

I often wonder why it is that most of us, for most of our lives, are looking to everyone else to give us clues and cues about what we ought to do. I've got news for you. God wants us to get our clues and cues from Him. He's looking for a man or woman who will stand in the gap and build up the wall. He will use you. He will use you on your job. He will use you in your family. He will use you in your church. *But I guarantee that He will ask you to do something that you don't think you can do and you are afraid to do or that you simply don't want to do.* Yet the moment you step out in radical faith, you will be empowered by Him. You will look over your shoulder and people will be following you. That's how life changes. That's how movements start. But how do we get there?

## HOW TO DEVELOP RADICAL FAITH

I don't know about you, but when I begin to seriously consider what a radical step of faith might look like, I get scared. Even after twenty-five years as a pastor and having seen God work in amazing ways, I still find myself fighting overwhelming emotions of fear when "that radical step" God is requesting becomes clear. Yet, I've come to the firm conviction that God is going to use someone, somewhere, to somehow fulfill His divine purposes in every situation and that someone will be an ordinary person just like you and me. The only difference is that ordinary person will have the courage to step up and take a radical step of faith.

I have no idea to what extent God may choose to use my life, but I do not want to miss the part He has for me because I caved in to fear. Like a player in a big game I've told the Lord, "I've got my uniform on, shoes laced, and I'm on the field and ready to go. You tell me what You want me to do, when, where, and how long and (although it scares me to death), I'll do it!"

Risk, fear, and faith are the common denominators of those God finds great delight in and chooses to use. God's most frequent command in the Old and New Testament to those who change the world are two simple words . . . "fear not!" Those dreams and ideas that He has placed deep in your heart to be a difference maker, to right a wrong, to meet a need, to launch a ministry, to break a barrier, to reach some that no one seems to care about are all a part of His preparation of your life to fulfill your holy ambition.

How about you? What was going through your mind as you read the last two or three paragraphs? Did your heart begin to beat a little faster and resonate with what I'm saying? Did you feel a rush of spiritual adrenaline followed by some good old-fashioned fear and doubt? Did you say, "O God, I don't want to go *there*," because you already know where and what *there* might be? Did you feel a strange mix of excitement and conflict? Has God brought to mind dreams that have been suffocated by the busyness of life or common sense, or the play-it-safe messages we so often hear from well-meaning friends and relatives?

If you are a believer, there's something in you that knows there has to be more to life than living in a nice house in Comfortville. Having two cars that work, a great marriage, two or three kids, and being the "nice American family" doesn't matter much if we're hollow and empty and having no impact. There's got to be more to it, and you know it's the calling of God. If you've been a Christian very long, you've tasted it. Whenever He's used you, whether in a little way or in a big way, you have ended up knowing people you can look at and say to yourself, *That person or that family is different because of something God allowed me to do. He used me, a regular ordinary person like me.* There is something that explodes in your soul at those times, and you want more.

Well, that's how you were designed. God created you to make a difference in your surroundings, to penetrate your world. That is why you are called light. That is why you are called salt. You are related to Christ. You are a difference maker. The same power that raised Christ from the dead dwells in you. What it takes for that power to get out is faith. We think it takes working harder and trying harder. No, it doesn't. It takes believing. It takes trusting. *So let me give you four critical ways from Scripture to help you develop that kind of faith.* They each have to do with what we remember.

> **Biblical faith believes in a very specific God with a very specific character who has made very specific promises.**

### 1. Remember What Faith Is and What It Is Not

The Bible gives us a clear definition of faith. Hebrews 11:1 says, "Now faith is being sure of what we hope for and certain of what we do not see." I think we often have some misinformed ideas when it comes to understanding what it means to have to exercise biblical faith. Faith is not having some type of emotional experiences or mystical experience. Faith is not achieved by endlessly repeating, "I want to believe, I want to believe, I want to believe." Faith can be emotional, or it can have no emotion whatsoever. Faith is simply believing what God said and acting on the basis of what He said, because of His character and because He gave you a specific promise.

If there is no object of your faith, it's just faith in faith, or faith in your emotions, or faith in your experiences. That's not biblical faith. Biblical faith believes in a very specific God with a very specific character who has made very specific promises. Biblical faith is believing to the point of action. You can feel afraid and act, or you can feel unafraid and act, or you can feel confident and act, or you can feel a lack of confidence and act, but any of these can be the starting point of practicing radical faith. One thing I love about the Bible is that it is filled with people just like me—with all kinds of hang-ups and baggage—but they stepped out anyway, and God was gracious. They had different starting points for their steps of radical faith, but they stepped out and God showed up!

### 2. Remember How Deeply God Values Our Faith

Hebrews 11:6 says, "And without faith it is impossible to please God [not hard, not difficult, but *impossible*], because anyone who comes to him must believe that he exists and that he rewards those who earnestly seek him." When you have faith, you need to believe that God is who He says He is. That He exists and that He is all-powerful. That He is sovereign and that He is the Creator.

The world is not out of control. God is still in charge. He has a plan. You are a part of His plan. Not only do you need to understand that He exists and is in control but that He "rewards those who earnestly seek him." Many of us don't want to step out in faith. We think that if we get totally committed and abandon all, God will invariably require us to do some of the things we fear the most. Those not married are sure they will never get married. Those who have a nice home fear it will get taken away. Those who like where they live are sure they will end up in an undeveloped country halfway around the world. Those who hate snakes will end up surrounded by them.

Do you know from whence these fears flow? They flow from a negative, warped view of God. God rewards. He knows how you are made. He knows what will bring the deepest satisfaction to your soul. Will He test you? Yes. Will He give you integrity tests and material tests? Yes. But everything—and I mean everything—God does will be for your good.

God is good. In fact, there is only one thing more dangerous than a radical faith that steps out and does exactly what God wants. There is only one price tag that will turn out to be eternally higher than the price of following Jesus. That's the price of staying comfortable; the price of running your own ship; the price of keeping it where you can see everything and know what's going on; the price of being a good, moral, safe evangelical Christian.

Do you know what we unconsciously think God values? We think that God is primarily interested in our morals. We think God's ultimate goal for us is to have nice families, keep an external set of rules, go to church, and be pleasant people. We think the greatest evidence of Christian maturity is letting someone get ahead of us in traffic, being kind at work, and giving money to our favorite charity. Unconsciously, we think that our morality rather than our faith is what is most important to God. The fact is, there are cults and religions that practice high morality and follow rigid spiritual disciplines, yet have nothing to do with real Christianity. They follow a system of works and religious activities that have no power and load people with guilt instead of freedom.

The morality of these groups may be attractive, particularly if we think that these people represent the kind of life God desires from us. But I've got news for you. The best morality without faith will eventually be proved bankrupt. Impressive moral efforts by fallen human beings do not impress God.

So what *does* please God? Is it getting our moral behavior superficially impressive? Absolutely not! *What pleases God is when we exercise faith. Nothing more; nothing less!* When we trust God, our morality, our behavior, and our relationships will be radically transformed. But that's the by-product, not the objective. Trusting God—believing—is the number one priority on God's agenda for our lives.

### 3. Remember What Jesus Taught His Followers about Radical Behavior

In Luke 9:23–10:37 Jesus outlines His specific strategy for teaching His disciples how to live by faith. But read through any of the Gospels, and you will find that the number one priority of Jesus was that His followers would trust Him. The only time He ever rebuked them was for unbelief. I have never read where He said, "Hey, Peter, quit cussing!" Or, "James, get control of that lust problem!" Now, I'm sure Peter and James both had spiritual problems, because they were just like us. But the only time the Scriptures record Jesus' rebuking them was for unbelief.

*First, Jesus called His followers to a radical faith.* He asked them, "Who do people say that I am?" Peter responded, "You're the Christ, the Son of the living God." He had the right faith. Immediately after that, Jesus turned to a crowd and said, "If anyone [not just superstars, pastors, missionaries, or more spiritual people] would come after me, he must deny himself and take up his cross daily and follow me" (Luke 9:23). Crucify your agenda and your will and take up My will and My agenda, Jesus was saying.

Then He spoke about reward. Price tag precedes reward. "For whoever wants to save his life [do his own thing, his own way] will lose it, but whoever loses his life for me [radical faith] will save it" (Luke 9:24).

For be assured of this, He went on to say, "If anyone is ashamed of me and my words, the Son of Man will be ashamed of him when he comes in his glory and in the glory of the Father and of the holy angels" (Luke 9:26). Faith was not going to be expected only of Peter, James, John, and a few superstars, but from *everyone*. The expectation was and is that every single believer, in every age, would be called to abandon all and follow Christ with all his or her heart.

*Second, Jesus taught His followers that the secret to having great faith was the quality of the object of their faith.* The key to having great faith is having a big God. If God is all-powerful and truly compassionate, if He is truly good, if He can truly do anything, and if He truly loves you, then whatever He asks you to do will make sense.

For example, Jesus took three of His key men to the Mount of Transfiguration, and what did He do? He helped them see His real identity. It wasn't as though a light shone down from heaven, and Peter, James, and John said, "Wow!" It was that He unveiled His glory and the light came from within Him and He was radiating the glory of God.

Moses and Elijah stood on either side of Him. Peter didn't know what to do, so he opened his mouth, as some of us would. But in the midst of that, they heard the Father speak: "This is My Son, My Chosen One; listen to Him!" (Luke 9:35 NASB). What was God's message for the disciples? It was that whatever Jesus says, you can trust that you can do it because now you know who He really is. You don't have to be afraid—He's God.

A visiting pastor heard me speak on this point and shared a great story about the importance of the object of our faith. He was in Maine, transporting some young people to a camp in the winter, when they came upon a bridge that was out of service. They were almost at the camp, which they could actually see about half a mile away across a frozen lake. He immediately thought of crossing the ice. Although it was cold and probably the ice was strong enough to support them, he could also visualize the headline in the newspaper: "Youth Worker and 11 Children Drown." Deciding to test the ice, he went out alone on the lake, walking slowly and listening for cracking sounds.

He had gotten about halfway across when he heard a loud noise coming up behind him. He was almost too scared to move. As the noise got louder and closer, he just had to turn around. There was a fully loaded logging truck driving across the ice in his direction. The guy in the truck stopped, and the pastor asked if it was safe. The driver told him the ice was twelve feet thick and then kept on driving.

How much faith does it take to walk across the ice once you've seen a logging truck do it? That's what Jesus was getting at. You need faith only the size of a mustard seed. If you have a big God, life's obstacles look small. That's why we want to take godly risks; they're part of practicing a radical faith. The more godly risks we take, the more our capacity to believe and trust grows.

When was the last time you took a radical risk? When was the last time you took a godly risk with your time, or in a relationship, or at work, or with an unbeliever, or with your money? When did you last say in response to God's prompting, "I'm going to step out and believe—and if God doesn't show up, I'm in big trouble"? The times you did that are your best stories, aren't they? Yet I know lots of Christians who live five or ten years between occasions when they actually trust God in some specific way with their lives.

People may see you as a nice Christian and a good, moral person. You give a percentage of your money regularly, attend church, and even help out in some area of ministry. *But when was the last time you took a radical step where if God didn't show up, you were in trouble?* That's the kind of person God is looking for as His eyes go to and fro across the earth. He's looking for you.

*Third, Jesus didn't minimize dangers.* As Jesus was teaching His followers about radical faith, He was careful to point out that not only are there dangers when we *don't* take radical steps of faith, there are also dangers when we *do*. You may be one of those who have taken some significant steps of faith and then wondered why those around you hold back. Jesus warned that when you begin to get on the same page with Him with regard to radical faith, there is a subtle but potent danger. The danger is outlined in Luke 9:46–56, where Jesus teaches His disciples that when they take radical steps of faith, they will be tempted to compare themselves with others. He warned them of the dangers of misplaced boundaries, misplaced zeal, and the unconscious gravitation toward thinking that we are the "only people God really uses." As we walk with God in radical faith, we must be on our guard so that we do not compare ourselves with others. Comparison is always the road toward carnality, where the focus shifts from what God is doing to what we think we are doing for Him.

*Fourth, Jesus outlined the cost.* There's an interesting scene in this passage that shows us Jesus' responses to impulsive actions, actions that may look like radical faith but are just impulses. Someone said to Jesus, "I want to follow You; I'll follow You anywhere." Jesus said, "Foxes have holes and birds of the air have nests, but the Son of Man has no place to lay his head" (Luke 9:58). Translation? You don't know what it means to follow Me.

Jesus says to us today, "When you count the cost of radical faith, you can't hang on to your stuff. You can't trust in your 401k; you can't trust in your job; you can't trust in your home; you can't trust in your equity; and you know you can't trust in the stock market. Any security other than the security I bring is an illusion." A lot of us aren't stepping out because we think it may mean something bad for our future. But what do we really know about our future?

In this same passage, Jesus turned to others and said, "Follow me." Two men responded with something like, "I would like to follow you, but—" Now, that's familiar. It's exactly what we do and say to Christ. One wanted to go bury his father (a delaying tactic). Another wanted to say good-bye to his family. You can't hang on to stuff, Jesus pointed out, and you can't hang on to people. Your wife or your husband, if you are married, can't be the focus of your life. Your kids can't be the focus of your life. You can't say, "I can't move out of the area because my extended family is here."

Radical faith honestly shares with God about wishes, fears, and desires, but radical faith never gives ultimatums or conditions to God. Radical faith doesn't say to God, "I'll serve You with reckless abandon and complete commitment as long as I can set the conditions and boundaries of my service." If there is an area in which we American Christians have failed miserably, it is this one. I meet pastors, even missionaries, Christians workers, and fellow leaders in ministry who state categorically that they are looking for God's will in their lives but have set definite parameters on when, where, and how that can take place. Sometimes the parameters have to do with weather or family. Sometimes the parameters have to do with geographic locations or levels of income. Sometimes they involve specific job requirements or work environment. We will never experience the supernatural power of God and find the center of His will until we let go of people and stuff as the security at the center of our lives.

If another person—husband, wife, mother, father, daughter, son, aunt, uncle, close friend—has the priority in your emotional life over the Lord God, that person has become an idol to you. Does God want you to love, care for, and enjoy great friendships with those people? Yes. But He knows the priorities that lead to life and those that lead to death. No one else but God can occupy the center of life.

I don't know about you, but God has brought this issue to the surface in my life on numerous occasions. I don't think we ever grow out of the process by which we continually go back to ask, "Is my heart fully God's, or has it gotten attached to stuff or people somewhere along the way?" One of my most vivid memories was in my first two years as a pastor. I was struggling in a small church in rural Texas. We met in a one-room schoolhouse located fifteen minutes outside of a town of about four thousand that didn't have a stoplight. The salary made it difficult to live, and I honestly questioned whether we were going to make it from month to month. I openly questioned God about my financial future, wondering how I would take care of my family.

As I was going through some old files one day, I discovered my insurance broker's license. I said to myself, "This would be good to hang on to, because this pastor stuff might not work out; and if I can't pay my bills at least I'll be able to support my family." It seemed like a logical enough response, but God began to deal with me for the next few days. Statements consistent with His Word began to flow into my life, statements like, "It's a noble thing to sell insurance. It's a noble thing to sell cars. It's a noble thing to build houses. It's a noble thing to cut hair, or to love kids, or to be an administrative assistant, or even to be a pastor." Those statements are true. Whatever God calls you to do is noble. "But Chip," I sensed God saying, "I've called you to be a pastor. I take care of My own. Now, no safety net other than Me. Get rid of the license." So I tore it up and tossed it in the trash can, putting my past behind me. God's safety net has never failed. A radical faith means we simply cannot hang on to the past.

So let me ask you, is there a relationship, a circumstance, or an object in your life that keeps you from really trusting God? Is financial security or fear of the future keeping you from taking a step toward God that you know He wants you to take? Is there a relationship in your life right now that is more important than your relationship with Christ? Could it be that God is not using your life as you have dreamed because you are simply not in a position where He can use you? What does your safety net look like? Until you have answered those questions honestly, you will not have counted the cost Jesus told His disciples to count before they stepped out in radical faith.

*Fifth, Jesus demonstrated that radical faith is caught more than taught.* When Jesus chose His disciples, part of His purpose was that they would simply spend time with Him. Eventually, though, He sent the twelve disciples out, and they started preaching and healing, and casting out demons. The results were astonishing. They came back excited and said, "Lord, the demons do what we say. God is doing this amazing work!" Then Jesus pulled them aside and said, "Blessed are the eyes that see what you see. For I tell you that many prophets and kings wanted to see what you see but did not see it, and to hear what you hear but did not hear it" (Luke 10:23–24). He made the reason clear. What they had seen was based on the fact that they had stepped out and trusted Christ. They didn't really appreciate firsthand the spiritual resources they had until they were in a place where they had to depend on what they had been taught by Jesus and what they had caught from being with Him. What they were experiencing was the power of the kingdom of God made evident in lives that were stepping out in radical faith.

> People who don't know how to swim eventually have to jump in the water. Until we jump in the water, it's all theory.

The only way to develop radical faith is to start where we are. We have to jump in. God will show us what it looks like to step out for Him, but radical faith can only occur when we actually step out. The process compares to trying to learn how to swim by watching films and reading manuals while standing on the tiles around the pool—here's a picture of the freestyle; here's the sidestroke. We can read and study those diagrams, but my observation has been that the people who don't know how to swim eventually have to jump in the water. Until we jump in the water, it's all theory. Until we leverage ourselves, it's all merely intellectual assent.

It's all theory until we put ourselves in real-life situations where we can pray, "God, I could get fired for this. This is a strong moral stand, but what is happening is wrong, and I know radical faith would speak out." Do we believe God is big enough to give us another job? I don't know what area God is speaking to you about, but I do know that a radical faith is not about intellectual agreement with what ought to be done. A radical faith begins when you respond in a specific, tangible way to what you clearly know is the will of God, regardless of the price tag.

So let me ask you, could God be speaking to you about a radical step of faith that involves . . .

- speaking the truth in love even if it might damage a friendship?
- breaking up with someone you are dating because the purity of your relationship is outside the boundaries of God's will?
- humbling yourself before someone you have disliked for a long time and owning your responsibility for whatever conflict there has been between you?
- taking significant financial risk during your twilight years instead of banking on your retirement?

You see, ultimately it is our fear of rejection, our lack of confidence in God's sovereignty and goodness, and our concern over what people will think that keeps us from taking a radical step of faith. If we believe that God exists and that He rewards those who diligently seek Him, isn't He big enough to bring another person into your life if this friendship or potential mate isn't the right one? Couldn't God change the heart of your friend through your honest counsel if you shared what you knew really needed to be said?

Do you see what I am getting at? The only way to learn radical faith is to step out! Is it fearful? Yes. We will always struggle with the feeling that we are stepping out alone, but we are wrong! God is with us. He has more invested in your life than you can imagine. As soon as you begin to walk by steps of radical faith you will discover a new sense of God's companionship and presence.

And you will likely have a lot of other companions, too. God has your best and my best in mind. His eyes are looking throughout the whole earth to find someone just like you, in your situation, who is willing to take a step to represent Him honestly, lovingly, and winsomely. What would it look like for you to take a radical step of faith today?

*4. Remember That We Are the Products of the Radical Faith of Those Who Have Gone before Us*

Did you ever think about that? Did you ever think about the debt you owe to an unbroken string of believers who, in a thousand ways, across the centuries, have kept the gospel flowing until the living water entered your life?

Your church, be it an old mainline cathedral or a contemporary worship center, a stately country church or a downtown storefront, stands as a wood, brick, glass, and stone memorial to radical faith. Someone looked at an empty field or lot or building and got a dislocated heart. He or she envisioned a place of worship. No matter what the size of the building, the original dreamers were probably overwhelmed by the projected costs. If their dislocated hearts were genuine, their encounter with the impossible outlook and the impossibility-crushing God left them with a broken spirit. But at some point, someone with a radical faith stepped in.

Explore the history of your church. Discover the living and past saints who have stepped out in faith through the years. In our church, I make it a point from time to time to retrace some of the steps the congregation has taken over the years. So many have given so much over the years that we enjoy today. Their example challenges us to faithfulness and stewardship. We honor them not just by keeping their dream alive but by imitating their radical faith in our own time.

## RADICAL FAITH TODAY

A healthy, radical faith in almighty God is a continually expanding proposition. The more you trust God's leading, the more opportunities to trust will be given. Fortunately, God seldom tells us ahead of time just how far He will take us. Churches that take radical steps in mission and ministry find that God shows up, not only with the resources but with an even wider vision. Budgets of thousands become budgets of millions; a handful of unique, targeted ministries becomes dozens of vibrant opportunities to meet needs. A vision that barely includes the neighbor next door becomes a vision that sees a world full of neighbors.

A radical faith is rooted (that's part of what the root word, *radix*, means) in God. No matter how large a stage God puts you on, your connection must remain strongest to Him. You may be aware of having an impact on thousands, but your focus must be to please One.

I have watched, with a broken heart, many people who started out moving with radical faith lose their root-connection and then lose their way. On a number of occasions I received the counsel of "experts" who've strongly advised me and our ministry to take matters into our own hands. We've been warned of impending disaster if certain "proven" fund-raising methods weren't employed. When we have taken these things before God, we have always sensed that God wanted us to trust Him more than methods. Methods offer a temporary relief from fear, but at the expense of seeing God work in special ways. Living by faith is exciting and, frankly, incredibly scary at times. But when you take a radical step of faith in God, God always comes through. You know what happens then? Your view of God grows.

I'll never forget how God taught me this in my second pastorate. We, as a church, needed over $500,000 in less than ninety days during a very difficult building program. We had been in this place only six months before, needing $363,000 in less than forty days. God miraculously provided then, but now, only six months later, the need was greater and our resources were reduced. At the time, I was reading through the book of Isaiah and I remember writing in my journal one morning that God had spoken very clearly to my heart that I needed to relax on this one. I jotted down that I was merely to tell people the need and instruct them to pray. God had said, "Don't lose any sleep over this one; I'll do it."

I had absolutely no idea how it was going to work out, but from our earlier experiences I had the conviction and complete peace that God would provide. God didn't tell me any details but led us as an elder board to clearly take a "hands-off" position on this one and trust Him. We didn't launch a special fund-raising program or a capital campaign. We didn't make visits to major donors or send any special letters out. We prayed and encouraged others to pray. I was convinced that if all of us did what God wanted us to do (trust in Him), He promised that He would do it. It's not that we thought capital campaigns or sending out letters would be wrong; it was simply not what God instructed us to do in this particular season of our journey with Him.

By December 31, the deadline, we were just a few dollars short of that huge sum, and I thought, *Wow! God has really come through!* By then, I had some idea of God's method for that challenge. It involved sacrifice after sacrifice after sacrifice on the part of many people. In fact, there were no huge gifts; everybody had a small part. As one of the elders, I remember thinking and praying about our family's building pledge. Most of the elders ended up giving twice what they pledged. So did many people in the church. I remember one elder meeting in particular where I signed up to give a third gift to the project, over and above our tithe and missions giving. We had two kids in college at the time, and I remember thinking, *I'm signing up for this, but what about them? What about retirement? And how will we make it through the next year?* Yet I ended up putting both kids through college without debt. God took care of every other concern that might have kept me from stepping out with a radical faith. I can't even tell you exactly how God did it all—but He did it!

Anyway, the story isn't over. I hadn't yet learned the bigger lesson. I went home and told my wife, Theresa, "Honey, this is so exciting. The money came in!"

She answered, "Well, how much actually came in?"

I told her the exact figure, which was just a few hundred dollars short of the required amount, and her face dropped. She actually looked disappointed!

I said, "Excuse me. What's the deal here?"

She said, "Chip, we asked God for $500,000, not $499,700. How come we're short?"

I said, "Theresa, with these kind of numbers, you round up! This is not a problem."

Then she turned to me with that tone that always gets my undivided attention. Her clear and straight thinking is one of the things I love about her. "Chip, I don't believe God works that way. I'm going to keep praying."

Frankly, I walked out to return to my office with a little air let out of my balloon but still feeling pretty good. My last appointment of the day was with our bookkeeper, Doris. She presented me with the final financial reports for the year. When she set them down on my desk, she said, "Oh, by the way, we had a postdated check that came in late in the mail, and I've added it to the final amount."

Can you guess the final total? That last-minute check completed the amount on the nose! God answered exactly. When you take a radical step of faith in the process of growing a holy ambition, how do you think God will show you He cares enough to show up? Exactly!

## AFTERTHOUGHT

Before we go on to the next phase of holy ambition, I want to encourage you to pause for a review. Ask yourself, "Am I really living by faith? Do I have a dislocated heart? Do I care? Do I have a broken spirit? Am I dependent? Am I willing beginning right now to step out and believe what God said He will do even to the point of risk? Even to the point of great sacrifice?" Has God put on your heart a specific burden that may soon require a step of radical faith? If so, what is it? What will you do?

No one can tell you what radical faith will look like in your life. No one outside of God and His Word can direct you specifically. At this point in the holy ambition process, what we are most concerned about is what is happening in your heart.

Remember what I said was one of the saddest verses in the entire Bible? God said, "*I looked for a man* [or woman] *among them who would build up the wall and stand before me in the gap on behalf of the land so I would not have to destroy it, but* [get this sad, sad commentary] *I found none*" (Ezekiel 22:30). But the description doesn't end there. There's an ominous conclusion that describes what happens when God looks but finds no one willing to be His person for the times. "'So I will pour out my wrath on them and consume them with my fiery anger, bringing down on their own heads all they have done, declares the Sovereign Lord'" (Ezekiel 22:31).

We're living in a world that is warped and perverted and needy: societal chaos, a world at war, kids being abused, and spiritual and physical needs like never before. God is saying today, as He said then, "I'm searching for a man, I'm searching for a woman, and I'm searching for a student who will stand in the gap . . . who will build up the wall, who will make a difference, who will take a radical step and do something with his or her life."

I just received an e-mail from a young talented couple that put feet to their faith and stepped out to make a difference for God. They write, "During a *Holy Ambition* broadcast, Chip offered the challenge, 'Dream a dream so big that only God can do it.' This dare quickly became a catalyst in our faith lives and sparked a dynamic change within, leading to the necessity for us to trust God to the point of acting in a big way . . . 'radical' faith. After much intense, consistent, and purposeful prayer, God answered with the inspiration for us to create a musical theatre production company to win people to Christ through the arts, using mainstream media and pop culture venues to reach those whom otherwise would not be exposed to the gospel. And we feel that God wants us to fulfill this purpose in New York City, and so we will be moving there in (from California). Long have we wanted to apply our talents in the arts to reach a hurting world for Christ. Encountering the Holy Ambition teaching has blessed us with the spiritual tools to allow God to be the change agent in our lives, producing true freedom, clarity of purpose, and a profound sense of faith in Jesus. Sincerely, Chad and Annie."

I believe if we'll step out—not because we think we are special, but because of who God is and what He has promised—that God will show up! He will use you personally! He will move other believers to join you and do a work beyond your wildest dreams. That's what He's always done! If you step out in radical faith for God, you won't be disappointed.

## TALK IT OVER

**Question from Chip on the video:** *What is it that you're hanging on to? What person? What stuff? What past? What identity? What are you afraid of?*

**1.** Based on your personality, where would you put yourself on the following continuums? Share with the group your perception of yourself and ask for honest feedback.

Optimist ◄————————————————————► Pessimist

Risk
Taker ◄————————————————————► Non-Risk
Taker

**2.** Chip said, "Radical faith doesn't mean that you are not afraid. Radical faith just means that you are willing to act despite your fears" (page 76). Describe a time when you were afraid but moved forward in spite of your fears.

**3.** "Radical faith is choosing to step out to fulfill God's clearly defined will at possible great personal risk and sacrifice" (page 77). Using this definition, who are some people in Scripture who lived a radical faith?

**4.** Who would be an example of radical faith in our generation? How has their life inspired and impacted you?

**5.** There is incredible joy when you step out in faith and God uses you to make a difference in somebody's life. Describe a time when you KNOW that God used you to bless someone else.

**6.** Chip said that, "We think that if we get totally committed and abandon all, God will invariably require us to do some of the things we fear the most." He also says that those fears come from a negative, warped view of God. What is your view of God and how has your understanding of God changed over the years?

**7.** Where do you sense that God is calling you to take a radical step of faith and "stand in the gap"? What is your next step?

## LIVE IT OUT

**1.** When you get to the place of taking a radical step of faith, you may need to seek permission and support from those closest to you. Who is it that you need to talk with? Set up a time in the next couple of weeks to share what God has laid on your heart.

**2.** Get clear about your next step. Write it down and share it with a close friend and ask for their accountability and prayer as you move forward.

*"For the eyes of the Lord move to and fro throughout the earth that He may strongly support those whose heart is completely His."*

—2 CHRONICLES 16:9 NASB

# a strategic
# PLAN

the fourth condition in developing holy ambition

"Carpe Diem!" Awhile back, that slogan showed up everywhere. I saw it embroidered on T-shirts, stuck on bumpers, and silk-screened on beach towels. I heard this Latin slogan in conversations. *Carpe diem* means "Seize the day" or "Grab today!"

"Carpe diem" became a popular expression when it was used and explained in the movie *Dead Poets Society*. In that story, the phrase was used to motivate a group of private school students to get serious about life. Their teacher made clear that each day might be the last before death and worms, so best to "go for it!" The message obviously affected a lot of people. The reality of death often does that. But for Christians, although death is part of our realistic outlook, we are actually more motivated by life. Holy ambition is about more than *carpe diem*. It's about *Carpe Vita!* — "Seize the Life!"

Holy ambition is about living your life in a way that makes an extraordinary difference. When you die, instead of just being another person who passed through, you leave a legacy. Your life matters in the scheme of things. People have something worthwhile to say or something precious to cry about at your funeral. You leave an indelible, good mark on their lives.

It doesn't mean that you're famous; you don't have to write a book or have one written about you. But in the eyes of God and in the eyes of the people you were closest to, you were someone who made a difference. You were one of those people who didn't play it safe. You didn't live just for yourself. You seized the day. You grabbed life by the throat. You did something significant. I believe that deep in your heart and deep in mine is a passion for our lives to make a difference. That's part of what it means that we are made in the image of God.

It's almost funny how foreign expressions will catch our attention in a much better way, even though we've heard the same message a thousand times before in English. Jesus made some amazing statements about the reason He came. He even had His own version of *carpe diem*. Does this sound familiar? "But seek first his kingdom and his righteousness, and all these things will be given to you as well. Therefore do not worry about tomorrow, for tomorrow will worry about itself. Each day has enough trouble of its own" (Matthew 6:33–34). He also had His version of *carpe vita*: "I came that they may have life, and have it abundantly" (John 10:10b NASB). You were created to seize the day. We were meant to really live! If Jesus gives us both this day and life in all its fullness, then the best thing we can do is grab them!

## UPDATE

Each time we approach a new condition of holy ambition, we see how the previous ones have prepared us. The other phases of holy ambition remain with us. A dislocated heart has helped us realize that God has designed us to respond personally and significantly to some need in the world. Our spirits have been broken by recognizing that as much as we care about that need, God cares much more, and our only hope of accomplishing the wild dream that dislocates our heart is to depend fully on Him. That leads us to take a step of radical faith. We depend on God by stepping into the breach and taking a very real risk with no other safety net than God's faithfulness. Which brings us to the fourth condition, the creation of a strategic plan.

## A STRATEGIC PLAN BEGINS WITH VISION

If a dislocated heart, a broken spirit, and a radical faith are givens, vision represents a not-yet-given. Vision isn't looking at the problem anymore; it's dreaming and imagining what would solve or replace the problem if God, you, and others moved into action. If the need is a big hole in the ground, vision sees a beautiful building that transforms the hole into something useful, such as a basement and foundation.

As I have shared these truths with groups, I have often been amazed at all the ways God plants visions in people's lives. Often, they report that hints of a solution or a possible wild result begin to come when they first develop a dislocated heart. Others tell me that they were so overwhelmed by the dislocation of their hearts that they didn't begin to see a possible solution until their spirits were broken and God began to reveal His power in their lives. And I know of others who have told God they were ready for a step of radical faith and found that God responded by giving them a sudden, clear impression of the need met, the problem solved. I don't know what it will be for you. But I know that we have reached the next phase. If you don't yet have a vision for what God wants to do through you, it's time to ask Him for one.

> *Vision is a God-given burden to see what a person, a place, or a situation could become if the grace of God and the power of God were unleashed on them.*

Vision is getting the big picture. Vision is a God-given burden to see what a person, a place, or a situation could become if the grace of God and the power of God were unleashed on them. That's all a vision is. It doesn't mean your brain works differently from other people's. It just means that something happens inside of you and you see things differently! Vision most often crystallizes around some burden or need, and as a result you see single moms or abused kids or a workplace situation or something in your home that needs to be and can be changed. Vision goes right by the "how" for a moment and sees the goal accomplished. That's vision!

We can see how this worked in Nehemiah's life. He knew a couple of groups of his people had returned to Judah. They had gone to rebuild the temple and the city. They were supposed to reestablish the culture of God's people. That's probably what he imagined was going on. Then his brother arrived with bad news. In a moment, Nehemiah's mental picture of Jerusalem got trashed and replaced by toppled buildings, breached walls, and burned gates. But four months in prayer brought Nehemiah to the place where he realized that God could turn his previous vision of Jerusalem into a reality. It took a dislocated heart, a broken spirit, and a radical faith to get him to that place.

When Nehemiah prayed, he asked God, "What do You want me to do?" That is why radical faith isn't the first phase of holy ambition. You don't just jump out and do something foolish. You get a word from God. You claim promises from the Scriptures. You let God work in you. Nehemiah got to the point where he said to himself, "One of the things that's missing from the terrible situation in Jerusalem is that I haven't done anything yet. I've got to make a difference." Out of this he came up with a preliminary strategy—find a way to get help for Jerusalem. Go to the top; ask the king.

Chapter 1 of Nehemiah begins with an individual. All great movements do. When God does something great, He starts with one person who has an idea, a dream, a vision. So the real question isn't "What can one person do?" but "Am I willing to be the one person God uses to make a difference in my world?" A great movement never ends there. It spreads to a group. By the end of chapter 1 of Nehemiah we can see from his prayer that he has a small team of people praying with him. He knows that the next key player in the plan is the king. Finally, the movement spreads to the larger world. By the end of chapter 2 the masses have been mobilized to do God's will.

Nehemiah's big vision saw the city of Jerusalem gleaming in the sun, enclosed by walls and towers, with firmly closed gates. He saw himself there, participating in that great task. This vision led to the strategic plan for making that dream a reality. Nehemiah divided the large, completed vision into intermediate phases:

§ He saw the king helping in some way.

§ He saw the details and dangers of getting to Jerusalem with the means to help.

§ He saw the challenges of enlisting the people once he got there.

We know he saw these things, because he was ready to speak about them when the right time came.

## A STRATEGIC PLAN LINKS VISION TO REALITY

Do you ever wonder why it is that so many people, so many groups, honestly intend to do so much, yet usually accomplish so little? The answer is good intentions followed by inaction. I don't think most people approach life with the conscious attitude that says, "I'd like to waste my life. I'm going to get up today and blow the whole day off. I'm hoping to accomplish absolutely nothing of significance tomorrow; in fact, I think I'll just blow off the next decade or two and be a nothing and die." I think most of us have good but vague intentions, but we don't know what to do with them.

So how do we take a dislocated heart, a broken spirit, and a radical faith, and make sure that our good intentions and our God-given dreams actually turn into reality? *I'd like to suggest that the answer is creating a strategic plan.* Picture for a moment the three conditions we have already discussed forming a committee. Your dislocated heart, broken spirit, and radical faith hold a meeting to discuss "What now?" What they decide will be your strategic plan.

I hope you are tracking with me up to this point. This is a critical moment. If you really see a problem, personally or corporately, and you see the possible solution and start to get excited about it, let me tell you where many visions fade out. A vision is the picture of a preferred future, but for that picture to become a reality requires a strategic plan. Notice that I said strategic plan, a plan that involves a specific outline or game plan, but it is definitely not all the details.

## A STRATEGIC PLAN CHAMPIONS AGENDA

When you see a huge need or a great possibility and start to step out to meet it without a specific plan, the inevitable problems will quickly sidetrack you.

The obstacles will stop you. You will say, "This will take more time than I've got. This is going to take a lot more people than I know. This will take a ton of money. This is going to take space." You will look at your available resources, and do you know what you will do? You will say, "Forget it. It couldn't happen. God could never do it. What was I thinking?" Or you may decide, "Well, stepping out was a big mistake. Whenever all the resources come in, then I'll know God's in it and I'll start again."

> God supports the visions He gives. But you don't get to see it happen until you step out, until you champion God's agenda.

I want to tell you that just the opposite is true. In fact, most visions never get off the ground because we believe the lie that we need to see the "ways and means" before we can take action. We think we need to see the resources and how it's all going to work before we step out in a radical faith. Nehemiah provides an excellent example of how God does, in fact, make the vision clear and asks us to step out in faith before we have any idea of how the resources will be supplied.

So if your vision is going to be translated into reality, you need to adopt a strategic plan and you need to actually step out in faith even if you don't know all the details of how things are going to work out. This may sound crazy, but it's how God turns dreams into reality.

## Nehemiah

Let's explore Nehemiah 2:5–8 together to see how this works out in real life.

> I answered the king [remember, he was risking his life], "If it pleases the king and if your servant has found favor in his sight, let him send me to the city in Judah where my fathers are buried so that I can rebuild it."
>
> Then the king, with the queen sitting beside him, asked me, "How long will your journey take, and when will you get back?" It pleased the king to send me; so I set a time.
>
> I also said to him [notice how bold he was at this point—he got the go-ahead from the king to reveal the next part of his strategy—and note that he

had a strategy], "If it pleases the king, may I have letters to the governors of Trans-Euphrates, so that they will provide me safe-conduct until I arrive in Judah [he's made tentative travel plans]? And may I have a letter to Asaph, keeper of the king's forest, so he will give me timber to make beams for the gates of the citadel by the temple and for the city wall and for the residence I will occupy [he needs money and resources]?" And [he knows who gets the credit for success] because the gracious hand of my God was upon me, the king granted my requests.

NEHEMIAH 2:5–8

Did you notice in this dialogue with the king that Nehemiah had done a lot more than pray during those four months of waiting before God? When the king asked specific questions, Nehemiah had clearly done his homework. He'd developed a tentative strategic plan that included a clear timetable, the resources needed, and the first steps in the project. Notice also, that his plan was formed before he had permission to go or any of the financial resources to accomplish the vision.

Jesus was emphatic and the Scripture is emphatic on this great truth:

> Where God's agenda is championed,
> God's resources are channeled.

Nehemiah championed God's cause, and God's resources were channeled toward his endeavor. When God can find a man or woman, a church or group, or a student who says, "God, I will champion Your cause. I will trust that the vision You have given me is part of Your plan. It's Your will and agenda, not mine," God's resources and money will flow. God supports the visions He gives. But you don't get to see it happen until you step out, until you champion God's agenda.

### *The moment of truth*
In the fall of 2007, God made it very clear that the focus of Living on the Edge

(our media ministry) was to change. After traveling around the world as president of Walk Thru the Bible for five years and ministering to pastors and leaders in almost a hundred countries, I came to realize the greatest need in the body of Christ was discipleship. People were coming to know Christ like never before in church history, and churches were being planted around the globe, but individual believers were not becoming spiritually mature followers of the Lord Jesus.

As a result of this experience, I came to the absolute conviction that the focus of Living on the Edge needed to be about making disciples, not simply teaching God's Word via radio, TV, and the Internet. This change in strategy was clearly God's agenda for His church and a refined and new calling for us as a ministry. But it is one thing to change direction; it's quite another thing to be willing to step out and follow the vision that God has made clear.

This new focus on discipleship would mean shifting our resources from expensive media outlets to creating a very expensive, full-blown Web presence that didn't simply teach, but would develop an interactive process where spiritual maturity could occur. The r12 online strategy was birthed and a very clear definition of spiritual maturity was developed. We willfully moved away from our focus on an ever-expanding global teaching ministry to deepening and developing individual believers who would then multiply their life into the lives of others.

I do not have space or room to outline all the implications of such a move, but what I can tell you is that we put the entire ministry at risk financially in order to move in the direction that God has shown us. Although we were not abandoning the teaching ministry, we concluded God had a number of significant teaching ministries that He was using around the world, but there were very few cutting-edge models that would reach the next generation and use the technology that was rapidly expanding around the globe. It was a frightening and exciting time to shift our forces and to pray like never before, though God would provide for all of our needs.

One of our first major steps of faith was committing to help people get into an environment where real life change could occur. We knew that the hearing of God's Word was an extraordinarily helpful first step for becoming like

Christ, but Jesus' example and the commands of the New Testament make it very clear that significant lasting life change only happens in authentic community. With this in mind, we told our million plus listeners a week that if they would commit before God to launch a small group using our DVD series, The Miracle of Life Change (an expositional teaching on Ephesians 4 focusing on how spiritual transformation really occurs), we would give them the DVD series free of charge. We had never done anything like this in the past, but we reasoned if life change happens in authentic community and small groups is the format that Jesus used, then our commitment to discipleship must be lived out by a willingness to create small groups among our listeners.

We encouraged them to check with the pastor of their church and gave them significant latitude in terms of how to develop their groups; but it was an integrity and honor system of us simply taking their word that they had made this commitment before God. We didn't know what to expect, but we were shocked when seven thousand small groups were launched in October of 2008. DVDs were flying out the door and we made no financial appeal to offset the cost. All we knew was that our mission was to help people grow in Christ and that getting them into a small group with the biblical teaching of how transformation occurs was the will of God. There were no hooks, no "give to get" messages, simply a commitment to give them the resources at absolutely no cost if they would commit before God to take their family, a small group at church, a small group at work, or group of friends for ten weeks to do the Miracle of Life Change. I have to admit I was getting a little nervous as the cost of production, shipping, and handling escalated as responses poured in to our home offices at Living on the Edge. But I learned the lesson that Nehemiah taught so well—God's resources always flow toward His agenda. God longs for His children to grow to maturity. God longs for us to be in authentic community. God showed us a step of faith that He wanted us to take. And God not only launched over 75,000 people in small groups in one month, but He provided for our needs.

About three weeks after our October launch, Sandi came into my office to let me know what the results of the prior month were. Although we had not asked anyone to help support the funding of the DVD small group resources,

377 of the 7,000 people who responded voluntarily gave a gift and told us they would like to help out to offset the cost. The gifts were of a variety of amounts as different people were led by God in different ways. I can't give you the exact number to these days, but within a couple hundred dollars I can tell you our hard costs to send out the DVDs was $21,694 and the unsolicited gifts given by people that month to offset our costs were about $22,100. God's agenda was championed and God's resources were channeled. Little did I know that that would be the beginning of an entirely new focus of our ministry. In the last eighteen months we've launched over 25,000 small groups across America and places around the world and conservatively, have 300,000 people in small groups studying God's Word, sharing hearts, and experiencing life change. In fact, the multiplication of these small groups and the stories and questions from their e-mails was so prolific, that we were forced to develop a coaching and small group resource on our website. It was great to teach people God's Word, but it's even more wonderful now to see God's Word taught all around the world and now see hundreds of thousands of people connected in small groups doing life together and seeing spiritual maturity really occur.

That's how God works. He doesn't wait until someone solves a problem. *You step out. His resources will flow.* Without sharing numerous other stories, let me simply say that almost every step in the history of our church and Living on the Edge can be used as an example of the way God's resources flow to the places where His agenda is championed. God's provision will always flow when He finds a man, woman, group, or church who will champion it.

*But we also have to have a strategy.*

## A STRATEGIC PLAN IS SPECIFIC AND WELL-RESEARCHED

In the very early years of God's birthing Living on the Edge, I found myself in a luncheon meeting with two venture capitalists. These were very wealthy Christians who probably had what the apostle Paul calls the "gift of giving." I wasn't sure what would come from this meeting, but I asked our staff to pray, because the radio and church ministries were developing in some significant areas and would require sizeable financial support.

One of the men I was to meet with had the reputation of being a billionaire. This was a little intimidating. The other man had successfully launched three or four companies, sold them, and made millions of dollars. They were committed Christians offering their time and strategic financial savvy in Christ's service because they didn't need to make money anymore. They were Prime Movers in what's known as "half-time." They had decided to refocus their time, talent, and treasure to leverage it more fully for kingdom impact.

After some brief niceties, one of them turned to me and said, "Tell us about your life and about the ministry God has you involved in—the church and the radio program." For over an hour I shared my heart and my vision. These two men were on the edge of their chairs, listening intently and asking questions. I was thinking, *Why do they want to hear all of this?*

As we neared the end of the conversation, the gentleman who had launched the companies and was known as a start-up specialist asked a simple question, *"What's your strategic plan?"*

I replied, "What do you mean?"

He answered, "You know, your strategic plan. If you have this nationwide vision and God has opened up all these doors, how much money is it going to take in the next five years to make this happen?"

I sheepishly thought, *I have no idea!* So I said, "A lot."

He continued, "How many staff members are you going to need? What are your needs for space going to be? How are you going to build your infrastructure? What kind of accountability and support are going to be required?"

As his experienced exploration continued I realized these were good questions, but I didn't have a strategic plan. Not knowing what else to say, I finally responded, "Gentlemen, these are excellent and helpful questions about which I need to do some very careful thinking."

That lunch meeting was a turning point in our then radio ministry. I pulled the leadership team together and said, "Guys, we need a strategic plan." So we did what good and effective ministries do. We did our homework. We conducted research. We talked with the most respected and godly media ministries in the country and asked them for their wisdom and experiences. They were gracious and helpful. Over a period of several months we came up with a clear, specific strategic plan that outlined our costs, our needs, our staff, and the details of our commitment to broadcast in the twenty-five major markets in America, to be a catalyst in meeting the needs of Christians and helping them discover and fulfill God's purpose for their lives.

As this process unfolded, we learned a huge lesson as a ministry team: A *strategic plan is crucial because God doesn't channel resources toward vague ideas.* Although all the details are not necessary, the strategic steps of where you are going and how you plan to get there are an absolute essential for God to supply the resources to accomplish His will.

## A STRATEGIC PLAN IS BIRTHED IN PRIVATE

Until it has been created, a strategic plan needs to be kept to a relatively small group. Input may come from many directions, but a strategic plan takes shape most clearly in a person or a small group of people who have been prepared to carry out the plan once it's ready.

Nehemiah demonstrated this principle. Listen to the second part of his strategic plan. We know now that he asked the king (the first part of his strategic plan). He got the letter and had the Persian cavalry sent with him. When he arrived in Jerusalem he was probably the highest-ranking official who had visited in decades. The protocol alone probably had the city buzzing. But Nehemiah didn't demand fanfare or special attention. In fact, he did nothing public for three days.

> He went out and interviewed people all over town and found out the needs, the socioeconomic situation, and the spiritual climate.

Outside Nehemiah's lodging, people wondered what would happen. The word was out that a high-ranking official from the king was in town to do something about Jerusalem. The citizens must have been a little edgy. "Are we in trouble?" they asked one another. They began to think about their situation. Ezra, the godly scribe, had been in the city for some four years trying to preach but had gotten nowhere. Many years before, Zerubbabel had returned with a group and rebuilt the temple, but it wasn't being used and the people were not walking with God. They didn't honor the Sabbath or bring their tithes. Things were a mess, and now a heavyweight has arrived.

I don't know about you, but if I were Nehemiah, I would have called a press conference. My prepared statement might have read something like this: "Folks, there's a new sheriff in town. My name is Nehemiah, and I've come to rescue you. The king and I are tight. I have an unlimited budget. If you just listen to me I'll show you how to turn this thing around." Fortunately for everyone, that's not what Nehemiah did. Notice how his strategic plan actually developed.

> I went to Jerusalem, and after staying there three days I set out during the night with a few men. I had not told anyone what my God had put in my heart to do for Jerusalem. There were no mounts with me except the one I was riding on. By night I went out through the Valley Gate toward the Jackal Well and the Dung Gate, examining the walls of Jerusalem, which had been broken down, and its gates, which had been destroyed by fire. Then I moved on toward the Fountain Gate and the King's Pool, but there was not enough room for my mount to get through; so I went up the valley by night, examining the wall [notice that he used the word *examining* twice in describing his purpose. Like a surgeon probing a wound, Nehemiah carefully catalogued the extent of the damage]. Finally, I turned back and reentered through the Valley Gate. The officials did not know where I had gone or what I was doing, because as yet I had said nothing to the Jews or the priests or nobles or officials or any others who would be doing the work.
>
> NEHEMIAH 2:11–16

Do you get what he did here? No big announcement, no press conference, no banners, no flyers, no PowerPoint presentations. He just walked around and found out what was going on. He went out and interviewed people all over town and found out the needs, the socioeconomic situation, and the spiritual climate. It was all hands-on research, done quietly.

Can you imagine what the scene might have been like? Nehemiah was probably holed up in a downtown hotel in Jerusalem. He had a small, handpicked staff coming and going with reports. Nehemiah heard their findings, and the group began to make their assessments and to strategize. Although we don't have the minutes of those lengthy brainstorming sessions, we know the results. I can hear them talking about the wall, the gates, and the extent of the damage. I can almost see Nehemiah asking penetrating questions of his staff about the social and spiritual environment of the city. "Who is with us? Who is against us? Who has the power? Who has the influence? Where will resistance likely come from?"

I can also imagine the tone of the comments as the staff returned from their fact-finding missions.

"Well, we have a lot of structural damage over here and a lot of fire damage over there," the engineer reported.

One observer of the social structure commented, "I think the power players and the influencers among the nobles and the Jews are over there. We've got leadership groups over here. It seems like there's a real leadership vacuum over there on the south side of town."

Nehemiah listened and evaluated the whole picture. Then, in the Jerusalem Hotel room (yes, I know I'm embellishing the story a bit, but bear with me), they used a whiteboard to list the priorities, diagram the specific projects, and draw up a plan of action. Do you know what Nehemiah was doing? He was coming up with a strategic plan for this second stage of his work. He was saying, "Here is what we need; here's what we're going to do; here's how we're going to do it. Now, it's been three days and we've created a little curiosity. Let's launch the plan."

Nehemiah put the finishing touches on this strategic plan in three days and a night. Those hours were the intense culmination of more than a year of preparation. Things moved fast toward the end because the right kind of foundation had been established. The work God accomplished in dislocating Nehemiah's heart, breaking his spirit, and strengthening his faith to radical levels prepared the way for the strategic plan to be birthed.

*So how do ordinary people like you and me develop a strategic plan? We follow Nehemiah's example.* Note that during his first three days in Jerusalem, Nehemiah employed three specific tools. Those tools God will use to help you turn your burden and the vision He has given you into a strategic plan.

## Silence

The first tool is silence. When you create a strategic plan, begin with silence in order to listen. Once you sense that God has given you a vision to make a difference, don't go blabbing about it. Nehemiah didn't assume he had all the answers. He didn't assume he knew all the facts. He found ways to discover what other people thought. Nehemiah understood that he was a small part of a much bigger picture. You and I and whoever joins us are always just pieces of God's larger plan. Whatever God is going to do through your life, your family, or your church, you must remember that you are just a piece of a puzzle. That means you must listen carefully to what God is doing in the lives of those around you.

In most strategic plans, those people who have been burdened with the vision will be the primary catalysts, but they cannot accomplish the vision by themselves. That means they must listen carefully! That means that when you get excited, you must do the very opposite of what you want to do. You must be quiet, keep your own mouth shut, and listen to God. More strategic plans have fallen by the wayside because they were shared too early with too many people than for any other reason. Be silent! Listen to where others are coming from. Listen and pay attention to what God is doing in the lives of others and in the circumstances from which your plan will be birthed.

## Secrecy

The second tool of strategic planning is secrecy. As you listen, assess the situation and do your homework. Thoughtfully explore the need that dislocated your heart. Quietly become an expert. Don't just get emotionally excited and then try to get other people excited. Find out the extent of the need. Be alert for others who may already be responding or who have a dislocated heart similar to yours. Evaluate the available resources of time, money, leadership, and energy. What's it going to take? What's it going to cost? Who's in? Who's out? What factors are pluses for the vision? What factors are minuses for the vision? Don't take someone else's word.

Secrecy involves personal participation. You will want firsthand knowledge. Nehemiah got out there personally at night so that he could accurately assess the full extent of the challenges before him. He rode and walked the walls; he got "up close and personal" with the problem. Secrecy is essential for a thorough evaluation of the challenges and the possibilities. A strategic plan cannot depend on secondhand information about what really needs to be done. Unless you yourself accurately assess exactly what the problem is, what it's going to take to address the problem, and what resources need to be mobilized, your strategic plan is destined for failure. Secrecy is the time for honest, quiet evaluation.

## Solitude

The third tool for strategic planning is solitude. The purpose of solitude is to strategize, to bring together the results of listening and secrecy. I think there were times when Nehemiah took time by himself in his hotel room, or tent, after meeting with his small group. He got alone with God and prayed, "Lord, here's the vision I've got and the strategic plan that is coming together. I know You want to rebuild this wall. I know You want to restore these people. I know the 'what' of Your will, Lord, but now I need to know the 'how.'"

> There are times for discussion and information gathering, and there are times for solitude.

I can almost see Nehemiah pacing back and forth in his room, far removed from the crowd, looking over diagrams and blueprints, saying to the Lord, "Here's the situation as I see it. Here are the resources. Here's the handful of people with me. How does all of this work together to accomplish Your purposes? Am I missing anything?" There are times for discussion and information gathering, and there are times for solitude. Once you have gathered the facts, you must get alone with God and let Him direct you clearly and specifically.

To review, as Nehemiah was developing his strategic plan, he did three simple but fundamental things. First, he gathered a team to help him come up with a strategic plan. He knew God had a solution, and he also realized he couldn't discover it on his own. With this small group of people he engaged in a very specific approach to develop the strategic plan. They brainstormed; he listened. Second, he was secretive, in order to gather all the information without bias. Third, there was solitude, where all the information could be gathered with a small group of people to turn problems and challenges into God-given solutions through the resources and people He had provided.

As we study the results of Nehemiah's efforts we can see he accomplished three objectives:

1. He clarified the specific strategic plan.

2. He developed a means and a time to communicate the plan.

3. He identified the means to implement the plan (timelines, dates, needed resources, and key leaders).

We know all this, not because it is spelled out in the text, but because we can see the results in Nehemiah's actions. Although you may feel intimidated or overwhelmed by the prospect of coming up with a strategic plan, I would encourage you to follow Nehemiah's simple example. Strategic planning is not rocket science and it's not just for people a lot smarter than we. But it is one of the keys to moving beyond feelings, dreams, and intentions. Through times of silence, secrecy, and solitude, God will show you and a handful of others how to turn the vision that He has put in your heart into a strategic plan that leads to real needs being met and lives changed.

### A Life Lesson From Santa Cruz

Maybe seeing how this works in everyday life will help you get a clearer grasp of how to develop a strategic plan in your situation. At Santa Cruz Bible Church in the early 90s, we learned this quite by accident as we followed Nehemiah's example, though to be candid, we didn't exactly know what we were doing. We faced a problem just like Nehemiah's. But instead of having walls that were broken down, we had walls that were too close together. By that I mean that we were overflowing with people but had very limited space. We were already holding multiple services but couldn't keep up with the growth of the church. So we followed Nehemiah's example.

First, we began with a time of silence. We didn't debate or brainstorm a lot of solutions. We simply began to listen. Each of the ministers in our church was asked to provide an honest evaluation of the state of his ministry and the church at large. We invited the leaders in the church to do exactly the same thing. We didn't debate; we listened.

Then we widened the input by taking a church-wide survey to discern what were the strengths and the weaknesses of our church. We wanted to examine not only the obvious space needs but also other needs that might not be so obvious. We wanted to get as clear a picture as possible of the good things God was doing as well as other areas that needed to be addressed. So, like Nehemiah, we were quiet. We listened. We wanted to hear God's voice.

Next came phase two, secrecy. Like Nehemiah, we realized that we needed to stop, take a step back, and evaluate the information we had gathered. The core leadership team of the church got away to pray and to process the results of our listening. Twelve of us got together at a cheap hotel for two and a half days of roundtable conversations, evaluation, and prayer.

I'll never forget the last evening together. After talking and examining the needs of our church from every possible angle, we came to a point of utter frustration. We were wondering how God could solve our current space problems and literally let us "get out of the box." All the ministry space we had at that time was a small chapel that was bursting at the seams. We had an adult building under construction that would be inadequate as soon as it was completed. Our space needs were crushing creativity and limiting ministry. The multiple services were wearing out staff and key lay leaders. We felt stuck, exhausted, and, by this time, desperate.

Right in the middle of an intense discussion about how to get the most use of our space, someone suggested that it might be better if we stopped concentrating on what we could do with what we had and started thinking about what God might do if we had unlimited resources and time, money, and staff. The almost instant transformation was amazing. It was a group experience of moving from a shared dislocated heart to a shared broken spirit. One moment we were burdened by our problems; the next we were lifted by the ultimate problem-solver. Our attention shifted from the problems we were facing to the wonderful, all-powerful, resourceful God we were serving. We had multiple times of prayer and worship.

I don't mean to make this sound overly simplistic or overly mystical, but it was getting away for a time of secrecy that was the key to God's working in us and turning the vision that He had placed on our hearts for Santa Cruz Bible Church into reality.

The great planning time came to a close, but it was an unfinished experience. I remember realizing that a strategic plan had to be specific. We couldn't just get excited about possibilities or even leave deeply encouraged and more committed to the task unless we had a specific plan to follow. It wasn't enough to say, "Let's reach Santa Cruz," or "Let's be a better church." We knew we had to be more specific. What would it look like if God showed up in ways beyond our wildest dreams?

I clearly remember that at the end of that meeting the discussion moved in a direction that made us all a little nervous, although the Spirit clearly confirmed that it was He at work. We knew we had to put a specific target on the wall, but we were leery of using a number. Finally, one godly man after another shared a number that had been on his heart that he thought was a genuine stretch but attainable with God's help. Little by little the group came to a consensus that God was telling us to reach and disciple five thousand people in the next five to seven years. We pursued this goal not with a focus on numbers or programs but with a focus on people. The moment we wrote "disciple 5,000 people" on the board, we had a clear target that forced us to develop specific plans with that goal in mind.

We decided to plan in reverse, starting with the ends in mind rather than the immediate challenges. We formed small task forces to plan for specific areas of ministry. We gave each task force a specific assignment. One group was assigned to solve our space problems—both immediate and long-term. One group was assigned to determine what staff we would need in the coming years and in what sequence they should be hired. Another group targeted our finances to figure out what resources we would need in order to accomplish our goal of discipling five thousand people. By breakfast the next day, we all agreed that the immediate need was in the area of leadership. We realized that none of the above could happen unless our leadership base was expanded and our leadership core was grown to a deeper level.

That breakfast turned into an unforgettable spiritual version of an NFL draft. We listed the top fifty leaders in the church and then used that list to hold a draft in which each task force identified and claimed certain people on the leadership list they felt would contribute to their particular area. Each task force leader was to ask the five or six people they had drafted to begin to meet regularly at 5:30 or 6:00 in the morning for a time of prayerful planning and leadership development. That kind of schedule helped us quickly discover the commitment level of each of those leaders.

> The real value of a strategic plan is not that everything works out as you have planned, but that it gets you moving in a specific direction with specific goals.

This process may sound crazy and perhaps a little haphazard, but that is how strategic plans often work. We didn't even know what we were going to cover with those leaders, but we knew we had to get those leaders together. We didn't actually know what kind of space, staff, and money would be required, but we knew that godly, gifted people, given the task, would figure out the details once a clear target was on the wall.

I share this story to encourage you. As you can see, strategic plans are not about fancy charts, PowerPoint presentations, or one person telling everyone else what God told him we ought to do. Strategic planning involves a dynamic, unpredictable process whereby God's people, who have dislocated hearts and broken spirits and who have taken steps of radical faith, come together in silence, secrecy, and solitude to design a specific plan to move toward a God-given vision. Many of the details will be filled in as the group moves out in faith. Much of the plan will be adjusted and changed along the way as further experience, research, and input by other leaders occurs. But the key is a clear target and a specific plan to move the core leadership toward that target. When that happens, God shows up in a major way. From that humble beginning we watched God bring thousands of people to Christ in the next ten years. We saw churches band together to reach our community, feed the poor, help HIV patients and runaway teens. God far exceeded our goals, but it started with a strategic plan.

The plan I just described was written on a small piece of paper with time-lines and target dates relating to what we were going to do and how we were going to do it. I kept that little plan sitting under the glass on my desk all my years at Santa Cruz. I'd like to say we followed that plan to a T, but nothing could be further from the truth. In reality, that plan simply got us moving in the direction God wanted. You see, the real value of a strategic plan is not that everything works out as you have planned, but that it gets you moving in a specific direction with specific goals that allow others to join you and where progress can occur.

So let me ask you, "What is your strategic plan for your life, your family, and your ministry?" I don't want to give the impression that strategic plans are just for churches, large corporations, or people with the gift of leadership. Theresa and I have struggled for years to apply these principles to our marriage, our children, and the personal ministries God has given us. We have developed a strategic plan to deepen and enrich our marriage. It involves a specific time each week to meet for regular communication and "life-coordination," as well as times to get away, just to be with each other two to three times each year.

We had a strategic plan for our children as they were growing up and now pray and plan about how to help them as they disciple their children. We regularly evaluated where they were emotionally, spiritually, physically, and academically in order to determine what we needed to do in the next three to six months to help them grow to become the people God wanted them to be. It's not that we had file folders filled with lists or rigid plans that we imposed on them, but we carefully talked through the needs of each of our children during every season of their lives and had a strategic game plan to help them to deal with the challenges they were facing and to help develop the potential we saw in them. It is today our greatest joy to see how each of our four children have discovered God's calling for their life and chosen to follow Him with all their heart.

## A STRATEGIC PLAN IS LAUNCHED IN PUBLIC

Whether they are personal, family, ministry, organizational, or even national, strategic plans are birthed in private but launched in public. You have to put your strategic plan into motion. Otherwise, you construct a worthy boat or ship in dry dock but never launch it. You can build a vessel to carry passengers through the waves, but it won't do that as long as it sits on shore.

Without a launch that brings the plan to the public, the original group gets all revved up and excited about making the plan and not committed enough to make the plan work. I don't know about your life, but mine moves so fast that if a strategic plan doesn't get launched and translated into my lifestyle and schedule quickly and specifically, no change occurs. A strategic plan isn't complete without a launch sequence.

So let's see how Nehemiah launched his strategic plan.

> Then I said to them, "You see the bad situation we are in, that Jerusalem is desolate and its gates burned by fire. Come, let us rebuld the wall of Jerusalem that we may no longer be a reproach." I told them how the hand of my God had been favorable to me and also about the king's words which he had spoken to me. Then they said, "Let us arise and build." So they put their hands to the good work.
>
> NEHEMIAH 2:17–18 NASB

Those few sentences summarize one of the great motivational speeches of all time. Nehemiah recorded only the outline. He told the story behind his arrival. He described the king's support. He explained the source of the stacks of hewn timber that were arriving outside the city. He introduced the military guard the king had provided, as well as his own key staff. But Nehemiah also told the story of God's transforming work in his own life. He recalled the heartache he felt so many months before, when the news of Jerusalem's condition had reached Persia. "I started praying about our problem," he told them. "Then a small cadre of committed people started praying with me. It got really exciting."

By telling the story of how God worked, Nehemiah gave his fellow citizens the time and opportunity to catch his faith. He made clear that the task they were about to undertake had the highest divine and earthly authority behind it. He closed his speech with a thundering challenge, "The condition of Jerusalem reflects on every one of us. Let's get rid of this disgrace by rebuilding the walls. We have the king's permission and God's promise that we can do this!"

Before we look at the details of Nehemiah's launch declaration, notice the people's response. They did not say, "Good, Nehemiah! You're the man! Go for it!" They said, *"Let us arise and build."* Something occurred during that speech that transformed Nehemiah's vision into the people's vision. They didn't yet know the details. Their spirits hadn't yet been broken. They didn't know firsthand how much God would make a way or how much radical faith would be required of them, but their hearts were dislocated and they were ready to join Nehemiah.

*What brings a congregation to say, "Let us transform our neighborhood or city. Let us be the kind of church and the kind of people who make a huge difference"?*

What happened in that speech? And what happened in those three days of modeling, relationship building, honest questions, and genuine listening that caused this speech to be the catalyst for a great movement of God? What components of that speech need to be present in any strategic plan launch to make it effective?

What brings a family to declare, "Let's change the way we live"? What brings a congregation to say, "Let us arise and transform our neighborhood or city. Let us be the kind of church and the kind of people who make a huge difference, not because of what anyone will think or what anyone will say, but because God cares. Let's do it because it's what God wants us to do"? We know that Nehemiah's presentation accomplished its purpose because his closing line describes what happened next. "So they put their hands to the good work" (Nehemiah 2:18 NASB).

*Nehemiah's launch of his strategic plan illustrates at least seven steps that contribute to effectiveness.* Others will not own or participate in the strategic plan unless they experience these steps. As you read through them, keep two specific areas in mind: (1) How do these principles affect the launch of my personal strategic plans (life, ministry, family, job, individual vision and burden)? (2) How do these principles affect the way my local church goes about its God-given roles? Remember that you are part of the body of Christ. The vision that begins with one person (Nehemiah or you) God may well use to move a church, a company, or a nation.

### 1. Clearly Define the Problem

We must clearly define the problem because people get used to living with mediocrity, sin, and tragedy. They just walk by hurting people. They no longer see a problem. They avoid facing the truth. To launch a vision, begin by clearly defining the problem personally and corporately.

Nehemiah's model fits any setting. At one point, early in our marriage, my wife and I sat down and we had to say, "We have a problem." Unresolved anger, lack of communication, baggage from our past, the overwhelming stress of seminary, three young children, and me working full-time and going to school full-time was creating a chasm in our relationship. We had to define the problem and say, "We can't keep living this way! We love each other very much, but there is growing anger and unresolved frustration between us. If we let them continue, they are going to destroy our marriage." Once we clearly defined the problem, it was then and only then that we were able to adjust our marriage strategic plan to go get help together to work on areas we had no idea how to address.

Whatever the size of the problem or need, it has to be clearly stated. Nehemiah gave the people the benefit of the obvious by telling them what they could see as well as he could—that the walls were down and the gates burned. His tone made it possible for the people to look around, nod their heads, and say, "Yes, they are, aren't they?" Nehemiah helped the people come out of denial and spiritual complacency by clearly stating the exact nature of the problem and its implications.

### 2. Identify with the Problem

People are more willing to own a problem themselves if they are given the opportunity to do so by someone who already owns the problem. To continue the illustration from the previous step, Theresa and I tried to focus on our mutual problem. We didn't say, "Hey, honey, you've got a big problem." We had already learned that accusations and blame don't move a discussion in the direction of solutions. Whether the problems involve a marriage, a family, a church, or a company, those who are willing to identify and clearly own the problems are in the best position to work toward a solution.

### 3. Propose a "We" Solution

Nehemiah didn't say, "Now this is what you ought to do." He didn't dump the problem in their laps. Nor did he announce, "I'm the king's right-hand man. I have a lot of manpower. Did you notice my entourage? Keep out of our way because I have come to save the day!" He didn't take either of those approaches. Instead, he proposed a *we* solution. Go back through the text and notice how often he used the words *we* and *us*. He said, "We're in this together, guys. This is what God wants us to do." The *we* automatically invites others to participate.

Again, Theresa and I would look back now and both say that our marriage has grown because we have found *we* solutions to our problems. She didn't send me for counseling—we went together. Children respond to training and discipline when they see themselves contributing to the *we* that represents the family. Those involved in ministry are likely to make amazing contributions when they participate in *we* solutions.

If you come up with a strategy to fulfill the vision God gives you, make sure that your *we* includes God. Since the whole objective is to accomplish something for God, it makes sense to remember that He is involved in every part of the plan. We won't make a difference for Him if we are not working with Him. We don't work alone.

When your strategic plan involves others, they need to own not only the problem but also the solution. Even if they haven't been involved in helping create the strategic plan, they certainly need to be involved in implementing it.

### 4. Give a Clear, Strong Challenge

Did you notice that Nehemiah didn't ask for help in a whining way? There's none of that "You know the gates are bad and I had to come all this way. It was a scary trip and a long one, too. I've got blisters. I've made all of these sacrifices and left my cushy job. Now, would anyone want to help on the wall?" He didn't manipulate; he invited with a challenge: "Come! And let's rebuild the wall."

If you want a big job done, it takes high-capacity people. These people are busy. They don't respond to pleas or manipulation; they respond to a big challenge that is tied to a large, God-ordained vision. Our problem is not that we ask too much of people but that we ask for too little.

### 5. Motivate at the Deepest Level

The motivation wasn't anything like, "We have gold bricks to sell and will engrave your names on them if you donate to the cause. We're also giving everyone noninterest loans when we're through here." Nehemiah motivated at the deepest level, called *intrinsic motivation*. This kind of challenge goes to a person's core. "Let us do a great thing for God. Let's leave a legacy with these limestone walls that says that God did something amazing here!" Basically, what Nehemiah said was *carpe diem*—seize the day! Let's be difference makers and see God's hand at work! *Carpe vita*—grab life! Let's be people whose hearts are completely His, the kind of people God will strongly support!"

### 6. Help Others See God's Hand in the Vision and the Success

After his challenge, Nehemiah reviewed all that God had already done by enlisting the king's help. He helped the people catch a glimpse of how far the vision had already traveled by the time it reached that day. Lots of impossible things had already become a reality! The people were being invited to join in God's great final push in this incredible task.

### 7. Explain Specifically How Others Can Be Involved in the Project

This step actually carries us into the next condition of holy ambition. It requires that we set the pace by defining our own involvement and then helping people define theirs. It's asking people to do what they can do as part of the adventure of finding out firsthand what God can do!

Nehemiah asked big things from people. He didn't ask for little commitments; he asked for huge commitments. He invited people to put their personal lives on hold in order to pursue God's objectives.

Scripture clearly teaches that Jesus did the same thing. He didn't say to the first disciples, "Fellows, could you come part-time or help Me a little when it fits in your schedule?" He said, "Leave your nets and follow Me." God hasn't changed. He is still going to ask us for a big commitment. You will stretch and grow. Sometimes it will get fearful and emotional. That is, in part, why developing holy ambition is a lifelong pursuit. It has various phases we repeatedly go through as God works in our lives.

I have seen this lesson work out time after time in my life and in the life of people and ministries all around the world. The cycle that includes strategic planning reminds us that God's challenge will eventually get very specific and very costly. I have witnessed businessmen and women invest their gifts and abilities for Kingdom purposes only after counting the cost and making significant sacrifices with their time and resources. I've seen busy people challenged to reprioritize their lives in radical ways. I've seen people step out to meet a challenge with resources I had no idea God had buried inside of them. But the process takes us through dislocated hearts to broken spirits and on to radical faith that creates a strategic plan. God uses that progression to prepare us for those moments of deep personal trust when we exercise the personal commitments required by holy ambition.

**Question from Chip on the video:** *If you have a vision (holy ambition), share what it is. If you still aren't sure, then share generally where you are burdened. Share what it is that you care about and find yourself thinking about often.*

**1.** Nehemiah not only prayed about the problem in Jerusalem, he came up with a plan. Read Nehemiah 2:5–8. What did Nehemiah do that was both strategic and savvy?

**2.** Chip said, "Where God's agenda is championed, God's resources are channeled" (page 103). Share an experience from your past where God "showed up" and channeled His resources to meet a need.

**3.** Chip said, "Until it is created, a strategic plan needs to be kept to a relatively small group" (page 108). What are some of the dangers of involving too many people too early?

**4.** Read Nehemiah 2:11–16. Once he arrived in Jerusalem, he spent some time probing the situation and examining the conditions. As you think about the burden God has laid on your heart, what do you need to understand further? What research do you need to do?

**5.** When developing a strategic plan "you must be quiet, keep your mouth shut, and listen to God" (page 110–111). How difficult is it for you to be silent? As you have been thinking and praying about the burden God has placed on your heart, what has He been saying to you?

**6.** Nehemiah was now ready to communicate the vision to the people of Jerusalem (Nehemiah 2:17–18). If you had 60 seconds to articulate your burden and vision, what would you say?

**7.** (page 118): "A strategic plan isn't complete without a launch sequence." Read Nehemiah 2:17–18. Notice in verse 18 that the people responded with the words "Let's START rebuilding." What would it look like to launch (get started) with your vision?

**8.** (pages 119–123): Chip outlines seven steps in launching a strategic plan. Which of these seven is something you do well and which of these seven is a weakness?

## LIVE IT OUT

**1.** Take some time this week to write out a concise and clear paragraph that captures your burden and vision. In your paragraph answer the following questions:

*§ What is the problem?*

*§ Why does this problem burden you?*

*§ What do you plan to do about it (with God's help)?*

**2.** Set aside one hour to just be silent and listen to God. Write down what He impresses on your heart during that hour.

*"For the eyes of the Lord move to and fro throughout the earth that He may strongly support those whose heart is completely His."*

—2 CHRONICLES 16:9 NASB

# a personal
# COMMITMENT

the fifth condition in developing holy ambition

---

Much of what we have discussed up to this point has focused on what God wants to do in us. Holy ambition involves continual personal adjustments, a growing awareness of the needs around us, a deepening acceptance of God's greatness, a strong desire to trust that God in the form of radical faith, and a strategic plan—all of which lead to significant inner changes in the way we live. But holy ambition is larger. Holy ambition looks beyond the delights and difficulties of having God do something very deep in us. Holy ambition is ultimately most passionate about seeing God do something through us.

I pray that God's Spirit has been doing real work in your life as you have read these chapters. I also hope that you are ready for the next condition of holy ambition. Jesus gave us a sobering picture of this process when He told His disciples,

"I tell you the truth, unless a kernel of wheat falls to the ground and dies,
it remains only a single seed. But if it dies, it produces many seeds. The man who
loves his life will lose it, while the man who hates his life in this world will keep
it for eternal life. Whoever serves me must follow me; and where I am, my servant
also will be. My Father will honor the one who serves me."

JOHN 12:24–26

Much of what we have been thinking about so far has been inside-the-seed work. God has been preparing you and planting you in His field. From this point on, however, the work of God in and through your life will definitely be bigger than you. It will require all of you.

## PERSONAL COMMITMENT

The closing ideas about the nature and importance of a strategic plan in the last chapter brought us right up to the next prerequisite in developing holy ambition: personal commitment. We will continue to follow Nehemiah during his amazing journey, drawing insights from his example along the way. Until this point in the process, Nehemiah largely functioned as the single seed Jesus described in the verses you just read. He was planted in Jerusalem and had done as much internal and private preparation as possible. Now it was time to do or die.

As he launched his strategic plan, Nehemiah made a personal commitment to join the people in the huge task before them. He wasn't just in charge; he was deeply involved. He put himself on the line to help a group of people that no one could get to work together.

Zerubbabel's past struggles and Ezra's recent frustrations indicate that the people had been unwilling to work or easily discouraged when they did work. Somehow, God used Nehemiah to galvanize His people in Jerusalem. Not just to start well, but to finish better. The key we're going to see is that every single person that day made a personal commitment. Not to Nehemiah, but to God. Nehemiah set the pace; the people followed.

As a result of Nehemiah's and the people's commitment, the wall around Jerusalem was rebuilt in fifty-two days. A wall many feet thick and many feet high, erected in a little over seven weeks. An engineering impossibility, I'm told. Yet, Nehemiah reported it in a matter-of-fact way, as if he expected just such a result. We read this account and are struck by the sheer boldness of Nehemiah's vision. How do we explain the results of his holy ambition? It turns out that Nehemiah's personal commitment provided a key component of what God wanted to do at that moment in history.

## WHY IS A PERSONAL COMMITMENT SO IMPORTANT?

Personal commitments bring awesome power. They are very powerful. Not just in the spiritual realm. Genuine commitment focuses and increases our attention on the challenge before us. We see examples of the power of commitment around us almost daily. Every time the Olympics are held we see athletes accomplish absolutely amazing feats and then discover during their interviews that these people have been working for years, sometimes decades, preparing for these moments, often measured in seconds and inches. That kind of dedication and commitment inspires.

### *Hoop Lessons*

I know this effect of commitment personally because it has had a measurable impact on my own life. When I was between the seventh and the eighth grades, I was five feet four inches tall and weighed in at 122 pounds — soaking wet. I wanted to be a basketball player. I was in a junior high of about seven hundred students and only Cindy Christian and Brad Star were shorter than me. The basketball coach gently suggested that I try out for the wrestling team. That was not a good sign of my basketball prospects.

One evening I went to a sports banquet where I heard coach Vince Chickarella speak. I had no idea how those hours would affect me. There I was, this young, tiny, skinny kid who was very short but who wanted to be a basketball player. Vince told two stories at the banquet that I will never forget.

One was about John Rinka, a player from Kenyon College who that year was leading the nation in scoring with 44 points per game. John Rinka's height was five feet, eight and a half inches. Vince described how he went with a football team up to Kenyon College for a game. On their way to the locker room, he noticed Rinka was in the gym, alone, practicing. He'd go to one corner and shoot and then to the other. He had chairs set up on the floor and used them as obstacles as he ran drills. The pace was not casual; every shot had the focus and intensity of a real game situation. The sweat was dripping off him. Hours later, when the football game was over, John Rinka was still in the gym, shooting, drilling, sweating. I sat there thinking and wishing that I was in Rinka's place, feeling the ball and hearing the echoes of the bounces, the baskets, and the touches in that gym.

*Whose flat-out commitment to some noble cause has inspired you?*

Vince also talked about a high school basketball player he had coached named Jimmy Clemson. Jimmy was cut from coach Chickarella's team both his freshman and sophomore years in high school, and was the last man to make the varsity team his junior year.

"During the summer before his senior year," Vince said, "I gave him three pairs of tennis shoes and loaned him two basketballs for practice. He wore out the shoes, and when I got the basketballs back, they were both bald. Jimmy went from last place on the bench to my star player." He told us that Jimmy went on to play at Ohio State University and eventually played in the pros.

Commitment inspires. I sat there in my five-foot-four-inch body listening to those two stories and I can't tell you how it worked, but a little light flashed on inside me. That night I walked away convinced in my junior high heart and mind that the only thing keeping me from my dream of playing college basketball was commitment. I decided to emulate the work ethic of John Rinka and Jimmy Clemson.

That evening marked a turning point in my life. From that day, a bad day for me was playing basketball for six or seven hours. On a good day, I had a basketball in my hands ten to twelve hours. Even when I was still, I did drills. I sat and dribbled. I walked and dribbled. When I talked, I dribbled. I played two on two, one-on-one, and even me and my shadow. I played with older kids and in inner-city pickup games. I played; I played; I played. I stood around basketball courts with that "Hey guys, I'll play" look on my face until teams let me be the last man. I wasn't proud. I begged. I played.

I was inspired to a level of commitment that actually protected me from a number of other influences. I never got into trouble or did drugs. I didn't have time. My basketball efforts ended up paying my way through college. The skills I honed during junior high and high school turned out to be useful when I became a Christian. I was able to play on a Christian team that traveled all over South America playing their national teams and sharing Christ at halftime. In 1978 I joined an Australian team and played throughout the Orient sharing Christ, meeting missionaries, and having God place in me a heart for the world. I don't doubt that I'm in ministry today in large part because of that commitment to basketball and the lessons I learned from it. So let me ask you: "Whose flat-out commitment to some noble cause has inspired you?"

## LIFE LESSONS

I ask that question because there's something uplifting and powerful that can happen when we rub up next to people who have made a personal commitment to pursue their goals. Their example can inspire us to greatness. Making those commitments ourselves protects us from taking shortcuts. They protect us from taking roads we shouldn't travel. By promoting discipline in our lives, they can protect us from developing character flaws.

*Making a personal commitment means we sign up in advance and say, "I pledge by the grace of God to do this."* Then, when we have a weak moment, we go back to that commitment and say, "I've already made a decision. I knew when I made that decision that there would be days like this. I made the decision anyway. I'm not going down that road. I'm not changing my mind based on how I feel this moment."

I can't begin to tell you how crucial this principle of commitment is for relationships. It creates the difference between a great marriage and a failed one. I think about my kids and Theresa, who by the grace of God is one of the most loyal wives in the universe. There's a fierceness and grace in her commitment that brings out the best in me. Our children are protected and provided for because there's something in our home called personal marital commitment. They know that come no matter what, their mom and dad are going to stick together and figure out how to work it out. We've had our share of ups and downs. But we have also been at this long enough to see how that kind of environment has helped our kids understand that our home is a safe place because we are committed. It protects us from bad mistakes.

Our children have also seen people give up jobs, marriages, kids, and other people, based on momentary feelings. We have talked about and experienced the truth in many ways that the temptation to give in gets strongest just before a breakthrough to deeper love, satisfaction, and understanding. People often quit just when things were going to get a lot better. Personal commitment can protect them until that time.

> *Until we put ourselves on the line and keep commitments, almost everything in life is cheap talk.*

Commitment inspires, protects, and also provides. It provides others and us with security and strength to reach goals and accomplish things we never could have otherwise.

*A commitment is a pledge or a promise. It's dedication to a stated course of action, relationship, project, or cost.* The word "commitment" may get used frequently in our day, but kept commitments are much harder to find. It's hard enough to get someone to commit to have coffee and then actually show up. People make commitment statements but don't really expect to be held to them. We are living in a world where people renege on their mortgages, marriages, kids, friendships, and commitment to Christ. Until we put ourselves on the line and keep commitments, almost everything in life is cheap talk.

The dynamic of personal commitment produces great things. We admire, long for, and want to be part of something that brings out and demands the best we have. But we aren't nearly as eager to accept the difficulties and costs involved in keeping commitments. I definitely know both the satisfaction of promises kept and the sadness of commitments I have broken. I have had my share of struggles and successes with diets, exercise plans, and devotional schemes. I have watched the pain in far too many marriages when commitments are broken and children search for answers from parents they trusted. Knowing how different those two results are drives me to do better and to wish better for you. I pray that the people in your life are experiencing the wholeness of the commitments you keep much more than the painful fragments of commitments you have broken.

## BACK TO NEHEMIAH

How is it that a man like Nehemiah walked into a situation where the walls were down, the gates were burned by fire, the people completely discouraged and yet accomplished one of the most significant feats in history? How did Nehemiah accomplish so much with so little? The key was not that he built a wall—that was just an outward expression of a profound inward change. The turning point was personal commitment. Until that point, nothing in the setting had really changed. All the dislocating, brokenness, faith, and strategic planning hadn't actually moved a single stone, built a new gate, or cleared away any rubble. What Nehemiah did after laying all the groundwork and depending on God allows us to see how God works in our world.

## WHERE PERSONAL COMMITMENT STARTS

Nehemiah realized that personal commitment always begins with a leadership. He modeled it convincingly. He didn't say to people, "This is what you ought to do. This is your problem." He knew that motivation is caught much more than taught. So he set the pace. He was sold out. He said, "You see the trouble we are in: Jerusalem lies in ruins, and its gates have been burned with fire. Come, let us rebuild the wall of Jerusalem, and we will no longer be in disgrace" (Nehemiah 2:17). The only "you" was an invitation to agree about the common problem "we are in." Every part of the solution depended on "we" doing something together.

Motivation represents only one of the lessons in life that is caught more than taught. Parents shouldn't expect their children to go beyond what they have seen modeled in their homes. In spite of everything we say to our children, they tend not to listen to our lectures that much. As a pastor, I know this is doubly true in my home. My children may not be able to quote last Sunday's sermon, but they do know my life this week. They probably won't remember much of what I say, but they will remember much of what I do. Kids catch what really matters to us. What they catch isn't what we say. What they catch isn't what they ought to do or what we think they should do. What they catch is the real you and the real me.

Nehemiah understood this principle. He modeled it convincingly. That was why he had credibility. That's why when he said, "Let's build," they thought, *This guy's going for broke. I think I'll get on his team.*

## WHAT PERSONAL COMMITMENT DEMANDS

Nehemiah made a specific personal commitment, and he asked for exactly the same thing from the rest of the people. One reason people around us don't get committed is because we hem and haw about how they can be involved. We say, "Would you kind of, want to, sort of, help out?" In our minds, we assume we're asking, "Will you be committed?" That's not what they hear. They actually hear lack of clarity, direction, and specific demands.

If they say, "Sure," they are probably saying little more than that they agree with our concerns and generally think someone ought to do something. Our nebulous request has gotten no more than an intellectual agreement. Any expectations we have that this person will actually take action in some way are almost bound to be disappointed. Why? Because we did not really ask them for a specific commitment.

Nehemiah asked for a personal commitment. "See those stones? See that gate? We're going to put things back where they belong. Come on, let's do it." When we ask people for specific commitments, do you know what we get? We get specific commitments.

## SUSTAINING PERSONAL COMMITMENTS

Emotional commitments often pass for personal commitments. Emotional commitments start well. They provide a rush of energy, but it proves short-lived. Emotional commitments are like the response to the gospel Jesus described in the parable of the sower as the rocky and weedy soils (Matthew 13:1–23). The seed of the gospel germinates, but it is withered by the sun of reality or choked out by the competition of other priorities and commitments. Emotional commitments don't last. Personal commitments may include emotions, but they involve a deeper level of decision making.

So how do we sustain genuine personal commitments? We can learn a lot from the weight control, alcohol resistance, and other recovery movements in our culture. They are often applying biblical principles that we are failing to honor in our spiritual lives. These groups ask for very specific commitments, but—and this is absolutely essential—they also provide an environment where others are struggling to keep the same commitment. Personal commitments are sustained by mutual accountability with others. When we have a bad day, someone else is likely to have had a good day, and vice versa, and somehow we help each other on those critical days that we are prone to drop our commitment. We all need that. Our culture may praise lone rangers who make it on their own, but Christians are called into a body, the body of Christ, and any personal commitment we make must be lived out in the context of authentic biblical community in order to survive.

If you long to know the secret of helping others (and yourself) make and sustain personal commitments, I invite you to examine the genealogies in Nehemiah 3 with me. Unfortunately, at first glance, this chapter doesn't look at all like an exciting passage of biblical teaching. The names seem unpronounceable, and the descriptions make little sense. Sheep Gate? Tower of the Hundred? Fish Gate? Jeshanah Gate? Doors, bolts, bars, and beams? This is the kind of passage that in our morning devotions or before we go to bed we might be tempted to skim over or not read at all. It looks like a list .

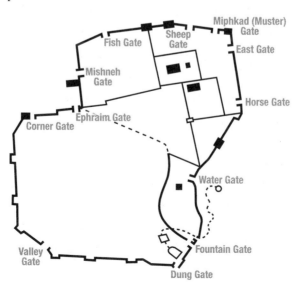

Actually, it *is* a list! What we need to know, however, is that the list has a beautiful order and structure. Some Bibles even have a picture of the city walls that helps us see the structure. If we take a pencil and read through the chapter, underlining each gate that is mentioned, we will discover a pattern. Notice also that there are key people—high priest, low priests, rulers, notables, perfumers, a merchant, and even a goldsmith—specific groups connected with each section of the wall.

This list takes us on a counterclockwise tour all the way around ancient Jerusalem. Nehemiah listed who was building walls, hanging gates, and repairing breaches in the wall. With meticulous accuracy, he mentioned who was working on which project, where they were working, and with whom. He also noted where these people were from. If we consult a map, we will discover that some of these groups came from as far as seventeen or eighteen miles away to work on this project.

This effort was not only designed to run like clockwork, but its success hinged on the gates. Every work assignment focused on a gate and its surrounding walls. Why? The gate openings were the most vulnerable places defensively. Gates also allowed access to the sources of water in an ancient city. The markets—the trades—were conducted and taxes gathered at the gates. The reinstallation of the gates brought a sense of order to every part of society. It announced that a government was in control. The elders who passed judgments and settled disputes met at the gates. The life of the city occurred at the gates. They were the points of entrance and exit. They allowed the city rulers to control who came in and who went out. So Nehemiah wisely made the gates his top priority.

As we can see, Nehemiah's approach was systematic and organized. Each group had a specific area of responsibility and certain duties: some built, some repaired, some hung gates, some worked on the walls. They always labored with someone next to them, a point that is made at least twenty-five times in this chapter. *In other words, Nehemiah's genius was to organize the people in family and ethnic groups for ease of communication and mutual commitment to see the work done. Each group "owned" a section of the wall.* The whole job moved forward simultaneously. They got synergy going. Some people may have had to work outside of their gifts at times, but every single person had a specific task.

Nehemiah also used the concept of vested interest in the way he scheduled the city people. Each group worked near their home (see vv. 10, 26, 28–30). There were two obvious reasons for these assignments. The first one was convenience. People didn't have to go far for their work on the wall. The other reason had to do with quality control. I don't know about you, but knowing an arrow or an enemy might come through the wall would probably inspire me to do a good job in front of my living room.

Nehemiah understood the wisdom of honoring protocol and position. His list of assignments began with the high priest. He got top billing but had real work to do. The key religious leader of the day was not Nehemiah, who did not even reveal his specific role. His job was to orchestrate. He developed an environment where the key religious leadership groups got the big picture and the vision. They coordinated the work in unity, and each person took part. As a result, experts say, the massive reconstruction was an absolute engineering miracle.

These walls were not like a wall in a garden, or a pile of stones between two fields. These walls were designed to support horse-drawn chariots. The huge stone blocks were often arranged to a height of fifty to one hundred feet and were thirty to forty feet wide. This was a huge task in any century! And Nehemiah's details in chapter 3 help us see how they did it.

## HOW TO MAKE AND SUSTAIN PERSONAL COMMITMENTS

There are at least three principles in Nehemiah 3 that can help us make and sustain personal commitments.

### 1. We Will Never Get Beyond How We're Getting Along

The first principle describes the importance of *cooperation*. Every task that occurs on this earth happens in the context of relationships. God has wired us that way. A vision will only be achieved to the degree that the people carrying it out really get along with each other.

Some of us get up in the morning and love to go to work. Do you know why that is? One reason is that we enjoy work when we are fit for it or good at it. Another reason has to do with relationships at work. When we walk through the door and find ourselves with people who we like and with whom we have team chemistry and energy, we look forward to work.

When the wake-up alarm goes off, some of us might not feel like getting up, much less going to work. Walking into a job and seeing this and that person who continually irritate us makes us want to turn around and go home. Negative conversations, backbiting, and gossip may seem to fill the air. We may feel surrounded by people choosing up sides in office politics and turf wars. What a mess! We never get beyond how well we really get along.

One of the greatest tragedies in the church in America and around the world is that Christians spend a lot of time and energy in conflict with each other instead of accomplishing the will of God. We will never be any better than when we work as a team. The principle of cooperation is what we need to apply in order to pull that off. How do we do that? We need to do what Nehemiah did.

Nehemiah realized that people he worked with were unique. In chapter 3 we learn that they all had different gifts, abilities, resources, and interests. Some people built from scratch; others liked to repair. Some wanted to work on walls; others worked on the gates. Everyone is unique. Others don't have to be like us. We don't have to be like anyone else. Life is like a huge jigsaw puzzle. We just have to find the spot where we fit.

Nehemiah understood the value of recognition in promoting cooperation. The immense worth of each person needs to be acknowledged in some way. The many names were not listed in chapter 3 by accident. Nehemiah could have said, "We built the walls and gates," and mentioned a few influential people. Not Nehemiah. Not only did he list their names, but he also included the names of their fathers. The names of their grandfathers and the towns they came from were often included as well. Nehemiah knew that 100 percent participation takes people knowing their role and being recognized in their role. That's why the great task was pulled off.

Nehemiah also helped people recognize that their common vision was greater than their individual differences. This group was a ragtag assortment of refugees and entrepreneurs. They were look-out-for-themselves survivors. We know from the prophets that many of those who had come back to Judah with Zerubbabel had stopped working on the temple and started building luxury houses for themselves. Nehemiah had to work with the second and third generations of these returned exiles.

Nehemiah cast a big enough vision to challenge and motivate them all. He told his story and stated his personal commitment. He didn't ask anyone to do what he wasn't already doing. And he reminded the people, "This is who God is! This is what God wants us to do!" He changed the course of history because his vision was bigger than "How does this work for you?" His vision was bigger than "What is in it for me?" His vision was "I want to champion God's agenda. Look at what God has done! Look at what God has done! Look at what God has done! Now, watch what God will do!"

Here's the application point: *Personal commitments are fostered when we feel like we belong.* That was Nehemiah's genius. He arranged and organized the work in that way, recognizing their uniqueness, the value of each person, and a vision. Every person felt he or she belonged and was making a contribution to the whole. The principle of cooperation works.

So how about you? Are you having trouble keeping a personal commitment in some area of your life? Does it involve work? School? Has the energy run out of a zealous commitment to a personal ministry that you once made? Do you find yourself with little desire to do what was once challenging, meaningful, and exciting? Maybe the problem is you don't feel like you belong. Perhaps some relationship building (or rebuilding) needs to occur before your commitment to the task can become a reality. Why not think that through, not only for yourself but also for those in your life with whom part of your responsibility is to help them keep their commitments.

Who in your relational network needs to learn to keep personal commitments, but just doesn't seem to have the discipline to do so? Could it be one of your kids, a friend, or someone at work? Ask yourself right now — how much do they really feel like they belong? How could you recognize the uniqueness of that person and let them know that they really have value to you and to those to whom they need to be committed? Do they really believe that they matter?

What specifically could you do or say to communicate to your friend, your child, or your mate that they really do matter, that you can't live without them. That there is a lot more at stake in their role in your family, at your job, or at your church than perhaps they realize.

It may seem counterintuitive, but relationship building is absolutely pivotal to people's personal commitments. *It is true: we will never get beyond how well we are getting along.* Whenever you see commitment failing in yourself, or others, check on the health of the relationships involved. Rest, encouragement, and affirmation may well result in a fresh surge of energy for the commitment and the task.

*2. The Combined Effort of the Group Is Far Greater Than the Sum of Its Parts*

Clearly, Nehemiah was a master in the art of coordination. He understood that coordinated people can sustain commitments. We can see this in his master plan for the wall reconstruction. The combined effort of the group is far greater than the sum of its parts. We call that synergy. In other words, it's not like one plus one equals more than just two. It's more like one plus one equals five to the tenth power. Somehow, as people work together and find their niche, the results are exponentially far greater than what we can do working apart. That's what happened when God put Nehemiah in charge and got these people working together. How does that happen? How does synergy occur? How does it happen in a group like this that we do way beyond what we could ever dream we could do? It happens in ministry just like it happened with Nehemiah. Here's how it happens.

## By recognizing that we need each other (Principle 1: Cooperation)

## By recognizing that there is a unique job for each one of us to do (Principle 2: Coordination)

Within the body of Christ, some people are builders. They build buildings, they build organizational structures, and they build people. Others find themselves drawn to repair ministries. It might be repairing people. It might be repairing things. Other people specialize in their gifts and find unique places of service.

One of the most amazing things I have discovered in the last twenty-five years as a pastor is how few people understand how God made them. Most people do not understand or know their primary spiritual gift let alone their personal strengths and weaknesses. It's very difficult to know how God wants to use you if you do not know who He made you to be.

One of the first things I did in my new role as senior pastor at Venture Christian Church, was to begin teaching on the topic of spiritual gifts. At Living on the Edge we created a small group study entitled "Your Divine Design" in which we walked people through a process of discovering their primary spiritual gift as one of the essential keys to coming to grips with the calling the Lord has on their life. It's been an amazing experience and joy to watch people in the church begin to look at themselves with a new lens. Here at Venture Christian Church we call it a "sober self-assessment." We're in the process of helping every member in our church discover their top three strengths, their top three weaknesses, and their primary spiritual gift. The Scriptures command us in Romans 12:3 not to think too highly of ourselves, but to think of ourselves with a sober judgment as God has allotted to each a measure of faith. The process of helping individuals come to grips with who God made them to be takes some time and energy, but it literally liberates people when they come to understand that they don't need to be like other people, but do what God created them and made them to do.

How about you? Have you found your niche in the body of Christ? If not, let me show you the beautiful and profound results this divine principle of co-ordination brings about.

One of the most powerful stories of seeing the body of Christ in action occurred a number of years ago when two young men visited our worship service. They wanted to encourage their parents to attend as neither of them had a personal relationship with Christ. So they invited them to the Saturday night service which was more causal, low-key and less intimidating to their folks who had rarely or never gone to church. The parents started coming. They began to show some spiritual interest, but did not have a personal relationship with Christ. During this time, the mom found out that she had cancer. It suddenly became a difficult and traumatic time for the family. God had their attention. He then began orchestrating a series of events, circumstances, and people in this family's life to create a beautiful and coordinated outcome.

> *This is how it is supposed to be! It worked because many ordinary people with wonderful gifts offered them to a family in need.*

First, a lady who attends our church was eating at the family's restaurant and found out about the cancer. She asked the mother if she would be interested in going to a cancer-related support group sponsored by our church. The couple reluctantly attended. Later that week they found themselves in a room full of fellow cancer patients and survivors who cared, understood, and prepared them for what was ahead.

Before long, the couple joined the support group, and it "just so happened" that one of the group leaders lived in their neighborhood. So once a week he went to the restaurant or their home and shared, cared, and loved them through the ups and downs of chemotherapy.

The cancer progressed. So did this family's dependence on God. Shortly after both parents trusted Christ, the mother went into a coma. The cancer support group gathered. Other church members arrived, including a musician with guitar. An elder and his wife stopped by. Then people started pouring in. Every contact point between the family and the church became a reason for someone to show up. The hospital staff had to create a larger space in the oncology unit to fit all of the people. For two and a half hours they sang, prayed, and worshiped in this double room with the woman in a coma. The hospital staff commented that they had never seen anything like it. Then, on a Sunday afternoon, she died and was ushered into the presence of Christ in her new eternal home.

Because of the family contacts through the restaurant, the church was packed for the funeral. I would say that about 80 percent of the people who attended the service did not know the Lord and had never heard the gospel.

Behind the scenes, other members of the church were busy preparing food, setting up chairs and tables, and finding ways to serve these strangers. I was amazed at all the ways these guests were exposed to the gospel many times before they ever heard the message at the funeral itself.

Often, when I share the gospel at a funeral, I find people quite resistant. As our culture becomes more and more secular, people not only don't know the Christian message but seem to wish the preacher wouldn't have to speak about sin, the gospel, truth, and the resurrection in the face of death. But this roomful of strangers was different. They were well prepared for the spoken gospel by the modeled gospel in the weeks before this woman's death. After the service, people walked up to me and asked, "Is this church like this during the weekend?"

I said, "Yes, it is."

They said, "And you talk just like that. You know, about life, death, God, heaven?"

I said, "Yes."

Their response was, "I'm going to come back."

Another man stopped to talk to me about the message, which had been based on John 11. As he shook my hand he said, "It's believing, huh?"

I said, "Yes."

"You mean it really is a gift?" he asked with a longing in his voice.

I said, "We're in the grace business, my friend!"

The entire event was a God-coordinated expression. The combined effort of the group far outweighed the sum of its parts. The impact was awesome. And as I leaned back against the wall at the end of the memorial service, it hit me. Every aspect of the church showed love to this family in its need. And, by God's grace, I had a front row seat to all this outpouring of care and concern that came through so many people in so many ways.

As I watched Christians loving in such unique and obvious ways, I teared up and thought, *This is how it is supposed to be!* It didn't work because it was a handful of high-powered players, highly talented individuals, or some big bureaucracy. It worked because many ordinary people with wonderful gifts offered them to a family in need. A handful of people who cared about cancer gave their presence, wisdom, and experience. Elders led, musicians played, and people who *could* be available *were* available to help in countless ways. That team produced a work for God.

Do you realize that God has a special job in Christ's body that only you can do? Can you imagine what would happen in your church or your home if every single person knew how needed he or she was to do "just his or her part"?

### 3. The Value of the Project to the Worker Will Determine the Value of the Worker to the Project

This is not just a clever expression; it's true. If the project means a lot to us, we will mean a lot to the project. If the project doesn't mean much to us, even minor obstacles, difficulties, or resistance will slow us down. Even a good game or an interesting distraction will reveal just how important a project is to us.

People remain motivated when they feel they belong. People remain motivated when they know they are needed. And people remain motivated when *the* vision of the group becomes *their* vision. Motivation begins with the leaders and influencers. Nehemiah chapter 3 lists quite a collection of leaders. The word *noble* is mentioned eight times. *Priest* is mentioned three times. Nehemiah understood that a leader cannot be a figurehead. A leader must lead. A leader sets the pace. As someone has wisely stated, "The speed of the leader is the speed of the team."

We cannot ask others to go anywhere that we won't go. There is probably no other area where we see the effects of this principle as clearly as we do in parenting. As noted earlier, our kids, like it or not, will not do as we say; they will do as we do. Unless we are modeling leadership in the values we say we believe and the commitments we make, we can be sure of one thing: our children will not follow. The same is true at work or in the church. Leaders must lead.

Jesus said it best when He equated leaders with servants. If, for whatever reasons, we happen to be people of status, wealth, leadership, or influence, that doesn't mean that we are of greater value to the kingdom of God. It doesn't mean that we are better than other believers. It means that we are stewards of certain gifts, abilities, and opportunities. We are going to give an account to God for our use of those things. If God has given us money, wherewithal, personality, or whatever, when we take a step we influence others. Whatever the size of the sphere of influence, God calls us to lead in it. Others are waiting for a challenge or invitation that God designed us to supply.

Although motivation begins with leadership, it doesn't stop there. Nehemiah points out that sustained commitment flows from vested interest. God understands our human hearts. All through Scripture, He talks about rewards. God's Word and promises not only bring glory to Him, but they also bring much good to us. We never serve God authentically and righteously with a "give in order to get" mentality, but God knows that when we have much at stake in a situation, we are then highly motivated to give our all.

We can see the vested interests in Nehemiah's assignments. He had people build the walls in front of their houses. You can imagine how much the motivation increases when the wall that you are building will protect your own family. He had people work in affinity groups where relationships were strong and the project would mean the most to that particular part of the community.

These assignments were not made off-the-cuff or without much forethought. This chapter is, in fact, very strategic. The completed wall would mean protection from enemies. The Israelites knew that the wall would prevent hostile forces from sweeping through and taking their daughters, their crops, and their very lives. These people not only had a renewed desire to serve God but clear and pragmatic reasons to build strong and straight walls close to their homes.

Beyond immediate safety, the completed wall represented hope for a better life. Once these walls were finished and the gates in place, they could get their lives back to normal. They could worship in peace and get on with their lives: raising crops, conducting commerce, and enjoying their families without fear of attack. They were thinking as they worked, *This will be good for all of us.* The way Nehemiah assigned them helped them keep their personal commitments.

## UP-TO-DATE APPLICATION

As we began this chapter we talked about the power of a personal commitment. It's not enough to get emotionally and spiritually moved and have a dislocated heart. It's not even enough to have a broken spirit and humble yourself before God, knowing that if He doesn't work, your labor will be fruitless. Nor is it enough to take a radical step of faith in God and step forward in the direction He has called. And, believe it or not, it's not enough to have a great strategic plan to channel your energies and dreams so that they can move from mere concepts and ideas to reality. The underlying essential condition that holds all the others together over time and against resistance is a personal commitment.

*There will be ups and downs and many struggles, but you will grow.*

*Life, impact, and making a difference are the result of people who make personal commitments and keep them.* Personal commitment is the difference between marriages that last and marriages that fail. Personal commitment is the difference between ministries that endure and those that end when circumstances become difficult. Personal commitment is the difference between staying in and benefiting from a tough course or quitting and flunking out of school. Personal commitments make it possible to stay pure and to resist the peer pressure when every fiber in your body wants to do what everyone else seems to be doing. Personal commitments, over the long haul, make up what we call character. When character, along with a dislocated heart, a broken spirit, and a radical faith, devise the kind of strategic plans that further God's agenda in the world, holy ambition has reached maturity in another life.

Let's think about your life. Where do you need to make a personal commitment? Not a good intention. Not a desire to try a little harder—but a personal commitment. That personal commitment will involve a place where you really belong, a supportive base of operations, where others can also join your efforts—*the principle of cooperation.* That personal commitment will in some way put you on a team, so that your efforts can be multiplied through divine synergy to make an impact beyond your wildest dreams—*the principle of coordination.* And that personal commitment must also give you a role in a larger corporate vision, deeply shared with others that it will be sustained over time—*the principle of motivation.* That personal commitment will give God access *to* your life to work *through* your life to accomplish, along with other lives, His agenda.

146

Nehemiah faced a city without walls, and he mobilized a group to make a difference. We are living in a culture without values and a church often lacking in principles. Will you be one of God's people to rebuild the walls? Will your life make a difference? Are you willing to pay the price? Will you make a personal commitment? If so, then holy ambition has taken root in your life. The conditions are developing in you that will allow you to make a difference in the kingdom of God. The eyes of the Lord are indeed going to and fro throughout the whole earth, that He may strongly support those whose hearts are fully His. He is looking for someone just like you.

Am I saying you need to be perfect? Absolutely not! But I am saying that daring to be available, getting clear on the vision that God has for your life, and then actually doing something about it is what this book is all about. It may well begin in your own family or with your own marriage. Maybe you have been putting off making it the priority it should be for way too long. Today you need to make a personal commitment.

Or it may begin with your relationship with God. You've read about a dislocated heart, a broken spirit, and a radical faith, but you know that those are only words right now. You need to make a personal commitment to begin to meet with God on a regular basis—to read His Word, to pray, to get into a small group, and to honor Him with your time and your finances. There will be ups and downs and many struggles, but you will grow. It all begins when you make a personal commitment.

You may also rediscover a dream that God has placed on your heart for years. Perhaps the dream has to do with the needs of single mothers, or inner-city kids, or some other forgotten or overlooked group of people. Meeting those needs would require something beyond your wildest dreams. But you have never gotten around to doing anything about that dream. In your mind, you have said you might get to it "when things slow down," or "when this or that happens," except "this or that" still hasn't happened. It's time to make a personal commitment to be a difference maker for God. Go for broke! Live with holy ambition! Don't hold back! Dare to live with godly reckless abandon! You will never be sorry. Misunderstood? Yes. Regretful? No.

If all this sounds a bit strong, a bit radical, then you are getting the point.

God doesn't use middle-of-the-road people who want to play it safe and are unwilling to take risks. He is looking for people like you and me: ordinary, available, consecrated people who are willing to make a personal commitment and then trust God to do His part.

I hope you will set the book down right now and do some quiet, reflective thinking. Personal commitments are holy moments. Scripture is clear: It is better not to make a vow than to vow and not follow through on the promise. But what a tragedy it is to be so fearful of making a commitment that you do nothing of real consequence or meaning with your life. *Ask God right now what personal commitment He wants from you—and then make it.* Bow your head right where you are and ask God to show you what His will is for you. And then, to use a popular phrase that actually fits well within holy ambition, just do it!

Now, as you pick this book back up, I pray that your will has been exercised. Your emotions may be anywhere on the charts, but commitments are about choices, not about feelings. But I do have a warning for you. Life may get a little tougher before it gets better. In the next chapter I want to talk about what will probably happen to you in the future. Genuine opposition will come your way. Your personal commitment will be tested, but God is with you. And He will not allow you to be tempted beyond what you are able to endure (see 1 Corinthians 10:13). You are going to make it. God is going to use you in a mighty way. But the way will not be easy. The final condition of holy ambition is a courageous soul.

## TALK IT OVER

**Question from Chip on the video:** *When it comes to your holy ambition what's your biggest fear? What's the thing that holds you back the most from taking the step of personal commitment?*

**1.** Nehemiah knew that motivation is more caught than taught. Who have you been able to watch up close and personal that was a person of "personal commitment"? How did that person impact you?

**2.** (page 134): Chip said, "One reason people around us don't get committed is because we hem and haw about how they can be involved." As you think about the vision God has laid on your heart, what is "one" specific commitment you could ask for from somebody else?

**3.** As a leader, how can you know whether someone is making an "emotional" commitment in the moment or a lasting, personal commitment?

**4.** (page 137): "A vision will only be achieved to the degree that the people carrying it out really get along with each other." How would you describe your leadership ability when it comes to building consensus and getting "buy in"?

**5.** (page 138): Nehemiah understood the value and importance of recognition. How would you rate yourself when it comes to generously handing out affirmation?

**6.** Think back over your own journey. When did you have the greatest sense of belonging? What was it that made you feel that way?

**7.** (page 148): "God doesn't use middle-of-the-road people who want to play it safe and are unwilling to take risks." Where are you playing it safe and you sense that God is calling you to take a risk?

## LIVE IT OUT

1. Intentionally go out of your way this week to affirm the people around you. Help someone feel like they "belong."

2. Take the time this week to write out whatever personal commitment God is asking you to make. Then, share that with a friend and ask for their support and prayers.

*"For the eyes of the Lord move to and fro throughout the earth that He may strongly support those whose heart is completely His."*

—2 CHRONICLES 16:9 NASB

# a courageous
# SOUL

the sixth condition in developing holy ambition

---

The best way I can honestly set the context for this final chapter is to tell an embarrassing story. I can only record this because the events happened more than two decades ago; otherwise I'd be pretty embarrassed. Now I can look back. I can see the lessons. Now I can see God's grace.

It was 1978 and I had made the deepest personal commitment of my life apart from my commitment to Christ. I had really done it God's way. After painstakingly making this commitment, I was discouraged, depressed, and disillusioned. I couldn't understand why God had let me crash and burn so badly.

I didn't come to Christ until after high school. I never opened a Bible until I was eighteen. Like most people, I made a lot of mistakes in relationships by not doing them God's way. By the time I met Theresa, I decided that we were going to do it God's way. For a period of about two and a half years, as we really got to know each other, we did it God's way. According to her, we never even had a date. She says all we did was sing and pray and read the Bible. I was so spiritual, she now admits it made her crazy. I decided that I would not even kiss her until I knew that I was going to marry her. I decided that we were going to be pure. And I actually thought that since we were doing it God's way, our marriage was going to be heaven on earth. She was the most committed woman that I had ever met. Then we got married.

At that point in my life, I was as committed to Christ as I had ever been, so my expectations about marital life weren't just big; they were galactic. Six days into our marriage we were back in this little apartment on the first floor of a rental house. I have no idea what caused the firestorm that broke out. I couldn't tell you any of the background details. All I remember clearly is that I was above the fireplace hanging a picture on the wall when something started. There was no fire in the grate, but hot words began to spark between Theresa and me. Soon, we had a verbal inferno going. In the next fifteen minutes she said things to me and I said things to her that neither of us had said before. I felt pain and inflicted pain. We had our first major fight.

> Over the years, I've been amazed how one or more of the conditions of holy ambition have triggered a response in someone's life that I could never have predicted.

I do remember very clearly the horrified shock I felt. I didn't think this wonderful, beautiful, loving woman was capable of such words and feelings. How could she do this to me? I was angry, hurt, and confused, so I finally just walked out the door. We had no clues about how to resolve conflict.

I drove in the hills over Fairmont, West Virginia, for two hours, thinking, *What did I do wrong? What's the deal, God? We did it Your way. Did I make a mistake? Did I marry the wrong person?* I actually thought this. I was completely disillusioned.

Looking back, I almost laugh out loud at my response to that minor issue. The very same kind of conflicts and sparks in our relationship more than thirty years later are like a bee bouncing off a windshield. No big deal. They don't even get on to the radar screen. The problem wasn't with our marriage; the problem was with me. My expectations were completely unrealistic and skewed. I assumed that we would float through life. I actually thought God owed us marital bliss because we approached marriage in His way. So when we had that first big argument, it was devastating. I, who had not expected to even stumble, found myself facedown in the mud!

I have since discovered there are specific measurements of the distance between our expectations and our experiences. If the distance is small, we call it a "minor adjustment." If our experiences are quite distant and different than our expectations, we call them "anger issues." If the distance is gigantic, we call it "disillusionment."

The last six chapters have introduced God-ordained conditions that affect the state of holy ambition in our lives. I pray and trust that you have been challenged to step out by faith and take some significant strides in your walk with Christ. You may have already made some decisions that will mean personal sacrifice for you and those around you. Over the years, I've been amazed how one or more of the conditions of holy ambition have triggered a response in someone's life that I could never have predicted. Careers have been changed, ministries have been born, dreams have been launched, lives have been transformed. I've watched great families and marriages get better and seemingly irreparable ones be saved as ordinary men and women followed God's call to holy ambition.

This book could have ended with the last chapter. After all, the condition of personal commitment puts a person in motion. But here is where we must be careful. To make use of my story above, the first five chapters deal with the dating and engagement part of a life of holy ambition. Personal commitment represents the point of promise in marriage. There's an aura of fulfillment, excitement, and anticipation in holy ambition that must be balanced by this closing chapter. Developing holy ambition does not mean a life of smooth spiritual sailing any more than preparing for marriage God's way guarantees no storms in marital life.

The common pitfall in both of the above cases can be found in the unstable soil of expectations. What I've learned from my own experience has been abundantly confirmed in the pages of Scripture. Whenever we step out and make a major commitment and say by faith, "I am really going to do it God's way," unconsciously we start thinking, *Well, since I'm going to do this God's way, life will probably get better. God is going to bless me. God is going to bring that special person into my life. God will be so pleased with my obedience that work will go great, my kids will do well, my health will stay strong, and my ministry will flourish.*

This thinking gets us into trouble. The truth is, God does what He promises, but we often misinterpret His promises. We want God to bless us according to our definition. God will, in fact, honor and bless our obedience and faith, but my experience is, *life usually gets harder before it gets better.* Why is this? Because our lives in their typical state are as shattered as the walls and gates of Jerusalem that Nehemiah saw as he approached the city. God's work in our lives isn't about paint and scrubbing; it's about reconstruction from the ground up, transformation, and radical renovation. Until Christ moves in, our lives represent enemy territory. We've been overrun and wrecked. The enemy considers us his spoils of war. The enemy doesn't yield ground easily.

Even when Christ takes possession of our lives, pockets of resistance remain. We don't invade or retake enemy territory, or deal with deep issues like lust, rage, sharing our faith, making major decisions, and addressing issues with our kids without running into serious opposition. We can say, "Our finances are going to get lined up with God's purposes," or "I'm going to get in the Bible for myself. I'm going to pray, get involved with ministry, address an addiction or a core area in our marriage, and so on," but the doing will meet with resistance. Sometimes, *fierce* resistance.

## INVASION TROUBLES

Whenever we choose to champion God's agenda, we are invading enemy territory. He doesn't go down easily. Usually opposition occurs first. When that happens, we get disillusioned and our first thought is, *What did I do wrong?* We didn't do anything wrong. In fact, if we go through the pages of the Old and New Testaments, we will find that every time a man or woman takes specific steps of holy ambition conditions get a lot worse before they get better.

Moses had a burning-bush call from God. How's that for definite? He went down to Egypt reluctantly, but willing to obey. What happened? God worked two or three miracles through Moses and his own people were ready to kill him. They said, "Moses, it was a lot better before you showed up." Opposition? Moses knew about that. He led God's people out of Egypt all right. They went kicking, screaming, and complaining almost every step of the way.

Elijah had a literal mountaintop experience where he stood up for God (1 Kings 18–19). Fire came down from heaven and consumed the soggy sacrifice. All the false prophets of Baal were removed. Almost immediately, we find Elijah running for his life. After his bold, radical, personal commitment to God's agenda, we find him exhausted, clinically depressed, and asking God to kill him. Elijah knew about resistance.

Jesus stepped up to do ministry and made it official at the time of His baptism. He heard His Father say, "This is my Son, whom I love; with him I am well pleased" (Matthew 3:17). Jesus was fully God, but He was also fully human. As a human, He heard the very voice of the Father in affirmation, "You've taken a great step." And what does the text say right after that? "Then Jesus was led by the Spirit into the desert to be tempted by the devil" (Matthew 4:1).

The apostle Paul had a miraculous conversion and began to preach. And what happened? Former associates tried to kill him. His former enemies had to save his life by lowering him over the wall in a basket (see Acts 9).

## TIMELESS AXIOM

When we take a step to make a real difference for God, here's the timeless axiom we can expect to experience: *Our greatest personal victories are almost always followed by periods of intense opposition.* So I thought I ought to end this book by preparing you for what's to come. If we take seriously God's challenge to live lives of holy ambition then we must anticipate opposition.

## OVERVIEW

In chapters 4 through 6, Nehemiah gives us a colorful catalog of opposition. No sooner does the task force swarm to the walls under Nehemiah's strategy than trouble rears its ugly head. In chapter 4 resistance comes in an *external* form. Chapter 5 ushers in another round of opposition, this time *internal*. The people start fighting one another. By chapter 6, it's *individual*.

Each of these chapters highlights a particular strategy Satan uses. In chapter 4, Satan's strategy is a frontal attack. By chapter 5, it's an unexpected ambush. Similarly, you may experience some problems in your family, problems in the ministry, infighting at work. By chapter 6, the strategy of the enemy gets very, very subtle.

Satan pursues his goal, which is to derail God's work, using a variety of strategies. In chapter 4 the goal is to discourage the people in order to get them to stop working. In chapter 5 the goal is to divide them. In chapter 6 the objective is to destroy Nehemiah.

Note also that Satan's weapons or means also shift, depending on circumstances. In chapter 4, Satan uses ridicule and fear to get the group discouraged. In chapter 5 we find him wielding selfishness and greed to get the people divided. In chapter 6, deception and intimidation are Satan's weapons of choice. *I seriously encourage you to make these three chapters of Nehemiah (4–6) a project for your personal Bible study.* As you travel down the road of holy ambition you will experience joy and rewards like you never imagined. But you will also face fierce opposition at every turn and in a variety of forms. You must prepare yourself for what is to come.

> **It is a noble act to step out and long to accomplish a great work for God.**

To help you get started, I want to arm you for what I think is one of the most difficult obstacles you will face in developing holy ambition. It is the natural opposition that comes from criticism, ridicule, and discouragement. So let's dig into chapter 4 of Nehemiah together and prepare ourselves for this first round of opposition. Then, I trust you will be able to make extended application in the following chapters of Nehemiah, using the same principles.

Remember, it's all about *expectations*. It is a noble act to step out and long to accomplish a great work for God. It is a foolish attitude to think that just because you do, things are going to be smooth, great, and wonderful in your life. As we begin our study of chapter 4, realize the lessons here are much like leaving a ringside seat and stepping into a boxing ring. You have the opportunity to make a difference in the cosmic conflict that is raging over the souls of men and women. You have been in training; now the fight is about to begin. Your opponent is a daunting one, and he will seek to destroy you in any way possible. Nehemiah 4 will provide you with a fight strategy.

## NEHEMIAH 4: HOW TO HANDLE EXTERNAL OPPOSITION

As I've already noted, I think the sport of boxing offers a good metaphor for the "blows" of opposition we experience as we progress into holy ambition. The apostle Paul uses it in 1 Corinthians 9, so I think it might be fair game as another illustration.

### *First Punch: Ridicule*

Round one: "DING!" The bell rings. Before the ringing fades we feel the enemy's first punch. When we move forward into God's program for our lives, we step right into the jab of ridicule and criticism. This is how chapter 4 of Nehemiah begins:

> When Sanballat heard that we were rebuilding the wall, he became angry and was greatly incensed. He ridiculed the Jews, and in the presence of his associates and the army of Samaria, he said, "What are those feeble Jews doing? Will they restore their wall? Will they offer sacrifices? Will they finish in a day? Can they bring the stones back to life from those heaps of rubble —burned as they are?"
> NEHEMIAH 4:1–2

We can almost hear the jeering laughter in the words. And Sanballat wasn't alone. "Tobiah the Ammonite, who was at his side, said, 'What they are building—if even a fox climbed up on it, he would break down their wall of stones!'" (v. 3).

These two adversaries understood the art of shaming. They didn't shout. They made comments just loud enough for their intended victims to hear. They asked rhetorical questions to the wind, but they fully intended to mock and humiliate the workers on the wall. Indirect but devastating, their comments meant, "You will never make it. You will never do it. You won't keep your commitment. You can't handle it. God is not in this."

Every generation has its Sanballats and Tobiahs. Every place where God is at work, the mockers and doubters come out of the woodwork. The comments may vary, but the tone remains the same:

- Do you really think that God is going to use one like you to make any real difference in the world? Come on — grow up.
- Do you really think that stepping out to share your faith at work is going to change anyone's life? You can't do it; you'll blow it.
- Do you really believe if you would work on your marriage, two months from now it will make any difference? He'll never change! That's just the way she is!
- Get a life. Your financial problems are so big you will never get out of debt. Why try?

That little voice, dripping with sarcasm, often comes from within. That voice can come from the enemy through your mind. It can come from a mate. It can come from a friend. But the ridicule that says, "There is no way you can make it," lands the first punch.

## Taking a Stand

I distinctly remember one of the early times I decided to do what I now call "flying your flag" — going public with my faith. It's that point in your life when you move from simply having private convictions about Christ to taking a stand publicly — even among those who may disagree with you.

My very first teaching job involved both teaching and coaching. And I decided that God had me in that school for more than just the intellectual education of those students. I remember thinking late one evening, as I instructed kids for hours in the fine art of getting a round ball through a hoop, *There's got to be more to this job than just this.* Because I desired to be involved in some kind of ministry in the place where I spent such a big part of each day, I talked with some of the kids and together we started a Bible study that met before school. (This wasn't a problem in West Virginia at the time.) Five or six of my basketball players started to come regularly. And God began to work in their lives. I couldn't help but see all kinds of possibilities. I wasn't nearly as smart as I was enthusiastic. I thought that God was just going to make everything wonderful (I seem to have this recurring problem).

One day, I walked into the teachers' lounge and overheard three or four coaches and one of the teachers huddled around a table after the women had cleared out. Lunch was over, and they began to talk in a loud and crude way about some of the more attractive female students of our school. I couldn't believe what I was hearing. I thought, *My mom and dad were teachers. I'm a teacher. I love teachers. Most of the teachers I know are great! Who are these guys? How can they sit here and make explicit sexual comments about sixteen- and seventeen-year-old girls whom they teach?*

I waited for some kind of indication that they knew what they were doing. No chance. The language just got worse and the comments became cruder. Finally I said, "Hey, gentlemen, I know that I'm the brand-new teacher here. I'm the youngest in the room, but what you are doing and what you are saying is absolutely unprofessional and uncalled for." I was on a roll and couldn't stop myself once I started. "Can you imagine being a father of one of these girls listening to how you are talking about them? I think this needs to stop."

It got very quiet. Before anything else could be said or done, the bell saved me and I left the room.

Before you could say, "Way to go, Chip," the jokes started. The teacher's lounge became a hostile place for weeks. Someone would begin a sentence and then stop, look sideways at me and say, "I guess I shouldn't say anything; spiritual Mr. Ingram is here." I got reaction from every direction. My colleagues seemed to turn on me. I stopped going to the teachers' lounge.

Why? I don't like to be rejected. I don't enjoy criticism. I don't like to be ridiculed. My reluctance to go to the teacher's lounge demonstrated the truth of the first phrase in Proverbs 29:25 (NASB), "The fear of man brings a snare." I was stuck. I felt trapped. I had to reverse my approach and start living by the truth of the second phrase of that proverb, "But he who trusts in the Lord will be exalted."

I began to experience some freedom when I realized that I had actually flown my flag and done what was right. God wants salt and light. Those challenges don't have conditions like "Be salt because the world will enjoy the way you taste," or "Be light because people will immediately thank you for pointing out evil or sin." Jesus' words "In this world you will have trouble" (John 16:33) suddenly had a familiar and personal ring to them. *So what if they don't like me,* I thought. *I can't control that. But they do need to respect me.*

I knew that my original comments had surprised them, but had been calm and direct. I had confronted the issue in as nice and winsome a way as these things can be done. Later that same day I had gone to each teacher and said, "I am not down on you personally, but I think this is inappropriate. I have real convictions about this." I tried my best not to be or seem self-righteous.

They had agreed privately. Approached alone, they knew they had been way out of line. But because of the way that they responded to me publicly, I had lowered my flag and fled. After ten days of avoiding the teachers' lounge I realized that I needed to return and live with the ridicule and criticism so that there would be a believing teacher in that place. So I went back. I didn't have to flap the flag of my faith in their faces, but people knew I had boundaries. I learned some valuable lessons about what to expect when we make a personal commitment to make a difference for God wherever we are. We can't predict what the price of obedience will be.

### Lessons from Nehemiah

Nehemiah's response to trouble offers us some excellent guidelines to follow in the boxing match of life. I hope the conditions of holy ambition that we have examined together have helped you identify and take some radical steps of faith. Are you getting a little flack? Are you getting a little ridicule or mocking? That flag of holy ambition that you ran up the pole in your life—has it slipped to half-mast?

*Here's how to respond in this situation.* Look at Nehemiah 4:4–5. "Hear us, O our God, for we are despised. Turn their insults back on their own heads. Give them over as plunder in a land of captivity. Do not cover up their guilt or blot out their sins from your sight, for they have thrown insults in the face of the builders." Nehemiah ended his prayer and continued his building report. "So we rebuilt the wall till all of it reached half its height, for the people worked with all their heart" (v.6).

Nehemiah's response to the first punch of ridicule and criticism was to pray. He prayed both defensively and offensively. He said, "God, hear me." He turned the offense of his opponents over to God for action. He felt free to make some suggestions to God about what He could do with the enemies, but Nehemiah left the doing up to God. He handled opposition by handing it to God. He let God take care of the defense of His people and the counterattack against the enemies.

I don't believe we should be paranoid, but if we aren't facing some kind of resistance in this world, we may be going the wrong direction. Opposition is actually normal. We should expect it. We live in a rebellious world. Satan never gives ground without a fight of some kind.

When we take a step for God in a loving, courageous, and winsome way, there are times when we are going to get flattened. Guaranteed. Many of us who claim to follow Jesus Christ aren't getting near the flack that God's Word tells us to expect. Why not? Because we are not taking the kind of stand for Christ that we ought. There are people close to us who don't even know we are believers. There are people who don't know our real convictions. So often, when something controversial or politically correct comes up, we don't say anything. Out of fear of rejection or ridicule we remain silent.

I've done it and you've done it. But salt has to preserve righteousness, and light must expose evil. We can't speak harshly, arrogantly, or judgmentally, but we have got to "step up" and "step out" and speak the truth in love. *We will never make a difference for God by doing nothing.*

Wouldn't it be powerfully freeing if we could get to the point where it's okay if everybody doesn't like us? Are we ready to accept the fact that representing Jesus will mean that others won't always accept us? Do we understand that it's simply not an option to be passive about things that really matter? If being a Christian means we will draw serious flack, let's just make sure it's for the right reasons!

## A COUNTERPUNCH

When I lived in Texas, my route from the outskirts of Dallas to a class down-town took me by a big outdoor drive-in several times each week. The marquee always announced in bold letters, "Triple X, Adult Movies!" I remember pray-ing, "God, this is poisoning people's souls." I inwardly hurt for the twelve- or fourteen-year-old kids who lived in that neighborhood. What damaging ex-posure from those images seen from a distance! They got the filth even if they couldn't get in to hear the sound track. Every time I drove past there, I prayed against it. I said, "God, shut it down." Like Nehemiah, I even added helpful suggestions, "God, please burn it down." Now, imagine how surprised and en-couraged I was when months later there was a fire in the projection booth and it burned down. The owners abandoned the property and a year later some-body bought it and started showing Christian family films.

Nehemiah reminds us that when we see the evil, whether perpetrated against us or not, our first response should be to pray, and God will answer. Our second response should be to keep doing what God has directed us to do. Nehemiah prayed, and kept the people working. He kept everyone clear on doing what they could do and trusting God for what He could do.

### *Second Punch: Discouragement*

The second major blow in this spiritual boxing match landed in Nehemiah 4:7–8. Not only were there the jabs of criticism but there was also the enemy's follow-up punch—the upper cuts of discouragement. In this passage we are going to learn that when God's agenda moves forward, the enemy goes from getting angry to being *very* angry. And when the jab of ridicule doesn't work, he will intensify his attacks through discouragement.

> But when Sanballat, Tobiah, the Arabs, the Ammonites and the men of Ashdod heard that the repairs to Jerusalem's walls had gone ahead and that the gaps were being closed, they were very angry. They all plotted together to come and fight against Jerusalem and stir up trouble against it.
>
> NEHEMIAH 4:7–8

When we take steps of faith, that's what is going to happen. Nehemiah's response? "But we prayed to our God and posted a guard day and night to meet this threat" (Nehemiah 4:9). We need to respond to attacks not only spiritually, but also practically. The threat may or may not be real. We need to prepare to meet it if it comes our way. That requires prayer and vigilance. Nehemiah's people did not let even the threat of violence make them swerve from their effort to carry out their purpose.

### On the Way to the Wall One Day

Verse 10 reveals a subtle complication that develops when people try to live in a state of high alert for a lengthy period. Fatigue sets in. People get worn out with constant watching and working. Among Nehemiah's task force, the slacking pace became the subject of conversation.

> The people in Judah said, "The strength of the laborers is giving out,
> and there is so much rubble that we cannot rebuild the wall." Also our enemies
> said, "Before they know it or see us, we will be right there among them and will
> kill them and put an end to the work." Then the Jews who lived near them came
> and told us ten times over, "Wherever you turn, they will attack us."
>
> NEHEMIAH 4:10–12

It isn't difficult to see what was happening. They were getting discouraged. I can almost imagine a conversation on the way to work on the wall. Two faithful workers, with their lunch pails in hand, begin to talk about their circumstances.

The first says, "Well, we've been through a lot. Do you think we can make it?"

His buddy answers, "I don't know. It's getting kind of tough. I mean, look at all this rubble! This is going to take forever."

"I know what you mean," agrees the first. "It was one thing when they were making fun of us, but, have you heard the latest?"

"No. What do you mean?"

After looking around, the first man says, "Well, there's a plot. The enemies are going to attack and wipe us all out with their armies."

"No, I hadn't heard about that," says his friend.

"It's true," declares the first. "In fact, it's all over town. Everyone is saying they're going to come in and wipe us out!"

The second man furrows his brow in concern. "What about our wives? What about our kids? You know, I was afraid this was going to turn out to be a dumb idea."

*If you are battling discouragement, it may be that you simply need to stop and rest.*

"Yeah, but we made a commitment."

"Well, forget the commitment. What good is the wall if we're all dead! Besides, I'm tired. I don't know how much longer I can do this."

"Me, too," agrees the first. "What do you think we ought to do?"

"Well, I'm going ahead to work today. But after today, I don't know if I can stay with this or not. This just doesn't make sense any more."

## FOUR CAUSES OF DISCOURAGEMENT

The pattern in Nehemiah 4:10–12 clearly points to *four causes of discouragement*. Each cause has a key word to help us spot them. The following sequence mirrors exactly how discouragement happens in my life and yours.

*1. Loss of Strength*

The first hint of approaching discouragement was a loss of energy. "The strength of the laborers is giving out," says verse 10. The key word for this cause is *fatigue*. Sometimes we start thinking that life is so spiritual that it's all about prayer and reading the Bible. But God did not make us just spiritual beings. God made us each a spiritual person, an emotional being, and a physical being—indivisible. We can compartmentalize all those factors to think and talk about them, but we live with all of them at the same time.

When we get tired, and I mean, flat-out, physically tired, something happens to us even though we might be right in the center of God's will. Days come earlier, nights come later, and the pressure rises, but you keep pushing ahead because you are doing exactly what God wants you to do. You are about to make a valuable discovery. It doesn't really matter if the spirit is willing if the rest of you can't keep up. Something begins to give. You become vulnerable and you get discouraged.

*Fatigue doesn't mean you've done something wrong. It may just mean you've done a little too much of what's right!* It doesn't mean that you are out of the will of God. It means that your body is tired; your emotions are frazzled. Welcome to the limits that come with living in a fallen world. Welcome to the value of the fourth commandment—where God orders us to stop, to rest, to Sabbath for our own spiritual and physical renewal.

If you are battling discouragement, it may be that you simply need to stop and rest. In our zeal to make a difference for God we can often become our own worst enemies. We start to live like we have no limitations. Yet Scripture reveals that even Jesus recognized His own physical and emotional limitations. John chapter 4 begins with a priceless description of Jesus that we often skip over too quickly. He was weary from a journey and sat down by the well outside Sychar. He basically said to His disciples, "Why don't you guys go and get some food in town? I'm beat." Jesus knew when to take a break.

Centuries earlier, the prophet Elijah (whom we've already mentioned) was in intense ministry and got so fatigued and drained that he developed severe depression and discouragement. By the time he took a break, he had become suicidal (see 1 Kings 18–19 for this story). He went from a great victory to emptiness because he was completely depleted physically and emotionally. And God's "spiritual treatment" for him was lots of sleep, rest, and a period of inactivity.

During my own seminary days I learned a valuable life lesson in this same principle. Not only did I struggle with expectations about life at seminary; I also got in my mind somehow that if I was really doing what was right spiritually, I ought to be able to handle anything life dished out. Now I know that is crazy thinking. This was my middle-of-seminary typical daily schedule: Visit the coffee shop from 5:00 a.m. until 7:30 a.m. to memorize Greek vocabulary; get in the car pool at 7:30 a.m. and go to classes; between classes, go to McDonald's and get a cup of coffee and read, read, read, every spare moment, between every class. At 5:30 p.m. I'd catch the car pool and come home and play with the kids for an hour or so before I left for work from 7:30 p.m. to midnight, after which I returned home to collapse in bed. Four and a half hours later I would get up and do it all over again. I did that for three years. I was young and strong then—driven and motivated.

Eventually, lack of rest caught up with me. One day during my third year I remember sitting about halfway down the banked seats in Dr. Charles Ryrie's theology class. Usually, the editor of the *Ryrie Study Bible* has some valuable things to say. I didn't hear his lecture at all that day. I had my eyes wide open. I was too tired to doze off. The lights were on, but I wasn't home. I was somewhere else, thinking that I had had enough. I sat there deciding, not just to quit the class, but also to forget the whole seminary thing.

"God," I cried out in the cave of fatigue, "we left West Virginia where our family was, our home, our life in exchange for this? This pace, this schedule, this mess? Well, this is insane. I'm working full-time, I'm going to school full-time, and I can't take this anymore!" I don't know what a nervous breakdown is, but it sure felt like I was on the verge of one. I was having this conversation with the Lord while the class droned on around me. I was in a stupor.

I didn't realize it, but the class ended and everyone left. They were kind enough not to interrupt my oblivion. Have you ever been in that spot before when you looked around and suddenly realized you were alone?

Dr. Ryrie is not an overly emotional individual. He's a very bright, clear, and compassionate thinker. I "came to" because I suddenly felt a hand on my shoulder. For a moment, he didn't say anything. When he did, it was the last thing I expected, but I'll never forget it. He looked down at me and said, *"Chip, go home and get a good night's rest or two. Get a good meal. Don't worry about your schoolwork for the next couple of days, and do not make any major decisions in the next few days."* Then he just walked up the stairs and left the lecture hall. It took a moment for what he had said to sink in. Well, when the man who writes study notes for the Bible tells you what to do, you listen. I thought, *I don't remember what I was supposed to do today anyway* . . . I walked off the campus, went to dinner with my wife, got some rest. A day or so later, I began to feel like I could make it. I've got the benefit of firsthand experience: one of the causes of discouragement is loss of strength.

## 2. Loss of Vision

This problem lies behind such statements as, "There is so much rubble. We're moving too slowly. We won't make it on time. We cannot build." The previous verses tell us that the wall was half built. The builders were already halfway to their goal. When they started, they were no-way to their goal. But they couldn't see how far they had already come.

The key word for this cause of discouragement is *perspective*. Almost all discouragement rises or falls with our perspective. The classic question of perspective is: Is the glass half full or half empty? Perhaps our challenge isn't as obvious as a wall. The choices remain the same. We look at all the rubble and wonder, "What needs to be done?" or "Look! It's half done!" Seeing what has already been accomplished can encourage. Looking at what needs to be done, especially when we're tired, leads to such comments as "Ain't no way, man. I can't make it!"

*If we focus on what's already been done and take a break to get refreshed, we give ourselves a chance to see what God is doing and to remember what He has done in the past.* That leads to confidence that God will help us in the future. We come out of discouragement. Loss of vision will make us lose perspective. Fortunately, as we will see in a moment, Nehemiah shows us how to get our perspective back.

## 3. Loss of Confidence

First they got fatigued. Then they looked at the rubble instead of the rising wall and said to each other, "We can't do this. We can't build that." Then they lost their confidence. They are certainly not the only ones. We can hear the same attitude expressed every day:

"I can't stay in this marriage."

"I can't deal with this child anymore."

"I just can't keep stepping out for God if I'm just going to keep getting this kind of flack at work every day. I'm going back to the old way of living. I may have lacked purpose, but it was easy."

The key word for this cause of discouragement is *unbelief*. Difficulties revealed the depth of their faith. It's interesting that when the wall wasn't built at all and they had a big God, they were ready and willing. Once they got tired and lost perspective, the focus went from upward and outward to inward and downward. The little self-pity parties started. Confidence became an endangered attitude. That leads to the fourth cause of discouragement.

### 4. Loss of Security

In Nehemiah 4:11–12 the people mention ten times that the enemy is going to come after them. Without strength, perspective, or faith, the enemy seemed invincible.

The key word for this cause is *fear*. Panic paralyzed them. God, Nehemiah, their personal commitments, their progress—everything faded before the enemy. *Why should we even build the wall now, they thought, since we're going to get three-quarters of the way done and they are going to swoop down on us and kill us?* They were badly frightened. With those fears, discouragement deepened. It was time for them to learn how to come off the ropes of discouragement.

## FIGHTING BACK

I don't know a lot about boxing, although my dad was quite a boxer in his day. I know that when a fighter is "on the ropes," or retreating, that's dangerous because he usually gets pummeled. What a fighter must do is get out of the corner and back into the center ring to regain his perspective.

Nehemiah may not have been a boxer, but he understood boxing tactics. He showed that entire group the way back to the center of the ring. They were tired, looking the wrong way, unbelieving, and scared to death—immobilized by discouragement—but Nehemiah led them out of the corner. He got them moving in the right direction. He demonstrated again the conditions of holy ambition. Difficulties just brought out the determination. When the going got toughest, Nehemiah got the people going.

God knew this moment would come, long before in Persia, when He chose and shaped the man He would use. Nehemiah got them to the place where they could see God the way he saw God. Nehemiah 4:13–20 describes Nehemiah's actions. Note how a real leader handles discouragement. He wasn't about to let his team go down for the count. "Therefore I stationed some of the people behind the lowest points of the wall at the exposed places, posting them by families, with their swords, spears and bows" (v. 13).

He started with positive and practical action. He knew that when all else seems to fail, people will still stand and fight for their families and homes. He put people in the gaps. "After I looked things over," Nehemiah followed up his first response with a quick appraisal. This was a leadership gut check. Like any effective leader, he was keenly aware of his surroundings—he made sure he knew exactly what was going on, and that others knew that he knew. "I stood up and said to the nobles, the officials and the rest of the people, 'Don't be afraid of them. Remember the Lord, who is great and awesome, and fight for your brothers, your sons and your daughters, your wives and your homes'" (v. 14).

> *Nehemiah responded to people's fatigue and loss of vision by changing their schedule and approach.*

What was he doing? He was giving them perspective. He named their fear and gave them the antidote. He told them all, "I know you're afraid. Get over it. You've got better things to think about, like your great and awesome Lord, and better things to fight for, like those you love." His words must have shocked the people like smelling salts under a groggy fighter's nose!

"When our enemies heard that we were aware of their plot and that God had frustrated it, we all returned to the wall, each to his own work" (v. 15). Most of us try to deal with discouragement by taking doses of distraction. We watch TV, or eat, or talk to others who often turn out to be as discouraged as we are. We need a Nehemiah in our lives (and we may need to be a Nehemiah for others) who will help get us moving. The opposition almost immediately looks different when we're moving toward God.

When Nehemiah took stock a few verses ago, he realized that 100 percent alertness wasn't practical for everyone. Less work would get done. So he made some adjustments. "From that day on, half of my men did the work, while the other half were equipped with spears, shields, bows and armor. The officers posted themselves behind all the people of Judah who were building the wall" (v. 16).

Nehemiah changed their work arrangement to keep both the watchers and the workers fresh. "Those who carried materials did their work with one hand and held a weapon in the other, and each of the builders wore his sword at his side as he worked. But the man who sounded the trumpet stayed with me" (vv. 17–18). They were all prepared to fight if necessary, but most were able to keep working.

But Nehemiah wasn't finished. "Then I said to the nobles, the officials and the rest of the people, 'The work is extensive and spread out, and we are widely separated from each other along the wall. Wherever you hear the sound of the trumpet, join us there. Our God will fight for us!'" (vv. 19–20).

Nehemiah addressed each of the causes of discouragement in the people. He responded to their fatigue and loss of vision by changing their schedule and approach. He reenergized them. He saw their loss of courage, so he refocused their faith. He recognized their loss of security and reminded them they didn't have to be afraid. He was even able to reawaken their sense of solidarity by promising a rapid response team. That's where that trumpeter came into the story. If any part of the wall sent Nehemiah a distress signal, he would alert the trumpeter who would sound the alarm for the armed forces to come running. "We're all in this together," he reminded them. "When any of us has a problem, the horn will sound and the cavalry will come!"

## FOUR KEY WAYS TO OVERCOME DISCOURAGEMENT

Clearly, the Holy Spirit was inspiring Nehemiah along the way. Because his heart was completely God's, we can see the evidence of God's strong support all along the way. The results make Nehemiah's life a pattern we can follow. In fact, we can take four principles from the passage we just reviewed that will help us prepare for the discouragement that will eventually threaten to immobilize our lives if we set out to make a difference for God.

### *Be Proactive*

When faced with discouraged people and discouraging circumstances, Nehemiah did two things. He did something practical and he did something positive. He took action and got moving. When we are discouraged, the most tempting but least effective response is introspection. Yes, there are times to think, ponder, and pray—times for self-examination. But there are other times to just flat-out get with it. When we start getting discouraged, we need to think of small, practical steps in the right direction. When we start thinking that there's nothing else we can do, we need to ask God to show us one more thing we can still do.

Nehemiah also took the positive step of putting the people into family groups. We respond the same way. We need to get around positive people when we start to get discouraged. Most people I ask agree with me that discouragement doesn't suddenly show up in life. We don't just wake up one day and say, "I'm really discouraged. I think I'll quit life." Discouragement gradually takes over.

In my life there's a little space I call "the gray zone." It's what happens right before full-blown discouragement arrives. I'm tired, lacking perspective, and thinking, *What's the use? I'm not yet completely discouraged, but like a fog making its way inland, I feel the loss of energy, a mild dissatisfaction, and a sense that I am headed for depression.* In addition, the gray zone almost always involves one little task or another. These are typical gray zone statements:

- I don't want to do the laundry—it's a job that never ends. I can't get ahead!

- I don't want to read my Bible—I don't get anything out of it anyway.

- I don't feel like praying—why should God listen to me?

- I don't think I'll go to church this weekend—no one will miss me if I'm not there.

- I am not going to get up and discipline that kid one more time—it doesn't work anyway.

The more of these kinds of statements we are considering at any one time, the larger our gray zone. We may not have decided exactly what to do, but these feelings and these thoughts keep coming to mind. *This is a crucial moment. If we don't keep track of the gray zone in us, we will eventually find ourselves in the pit of discouragement.* A tiny gray zone is part of living; a growing gray zone is trouble. That's not where we want to live. As soon as we sense the gray zone starting to grow, that's the point when we must declare, "I'm not going to be discouraged."

Most of us know that strange feeling that says, "Go ahead and sink into the gray. Don't even try to lift yourself up." That's exactly when we've got to do something. We've got to do it right away. It might be just getting up and washing the car. It might be just writing a positive note to someone. It might be just taking a walk. We have to shrink the gray zone by doing something very positive and getting around positive people.

But, instead of finding positive companions, we often do just the opposite. When we feel discouraged, we tend to get off by ourselves. Loneliness and the gray zone have a lot in common. Early in my Christian life, when I got discouraged, I stayed away from church. I didn't read my Bible. I didn't pray, and I didn't hang out with people who prayed. They made me feel guilty. Genuine, life-affirming people really mess up a gray zone. Those are exactly the companions we need! By the way, since I have become a pastor it's been really hard because I no longer have the "skip church option." I'm expected to be there no matter how I feel. Wanting to have joyful and Spirit-empowered Sundays in God's presence gives me a great incentive to keep a sharp, proactive attitude toward the gray zone in my life.

### Remember Who Is on Your Team

What does Nehemiah do next? He says, "Remember the Lord. Direct your attention to the Lord." What that does is get our focus off of the rubble and the problems and onto the solution and the One who can change things.

Unfortunately, I also know this from personal experience. I have struggled with discouragement. For some not-so-healthy reasons, I tend to get overextended. I get tired, so I lose perspective. I now have more than a twenty-five-year history of this battle with discouragement. One of the things I've learned is this: Remember the Lord! That's critical.

One person who knows me well recently asked me why I'm always looking backward and reviewing events before I begin looking forward. I told him, "For one simple reason—because that's when I remember the Lord." I do that in three ways: in meetings to help us all remember what God has done, in my journal a few times a week as I spend time with God, and spontaneously in restaurants on napkins and slips of paper wherever I am. Those settings trigger backward glances in my life, and I become aware, yet again, that God is always there!

I'll admit that there are many mornings when I get up that I don't feel like praying or reading the Scriptures. My life, like yours, includes a long list of tasks I don't always feel like doing, so I remember the Lord. For example, one Saturday recently, while the principles of this book were on my mind, I got up early and was alone with the Lord. I thought, *I'm going to write down my prayers because I'm battling discouragement and I need to remember the Lord.* But I also felt tired and overwhelmed. And then I thought, *Lord, I desperately need to get some perspective and focus on what You have done, not all I have to do.*

So I decided to practice remembering the Lord. I directed my attention to the Lord and wrote this prayer of thanksgiving: Journal Fall 2009

Father, I awakened very early this morning and feel totally wiped out. My body is still on East Coast time. Tuesday and Wednesday were super productive, but I feel like I'm running on fumes today. Help me get perspective, Lord. I have a lot coming at me and I'm battling low motivation and discouragement, so please help me remember how magnificently and generously You have blessed me . . .

- My sins are forgiven forever.

- Christ lives within me by the Holy Spirit.

- I am deeply loved by Theresa and my children.

- Your hand of blessing has been on my life, my children, the work of my hands, relationships, ministry, finances, and opportunities to honor that I certainly don't deserve and is far beyond anything I could have ever imagined.

- Venture Christian Church is growing more healthy every month. New people, many new Christians, finances turning around and a great staff coming together in unity.

- Friendships are beginning to develop.

- Theresa is being greatly used by You Lord, finding her role, getting connected with some quality women in the church.

- Living on the Edge has been blessed and used this year like never before:
  — TV launched through the Middle East
  — 22,000 small groups launched
  — TV in all Russian-speaking countries, Romania, Turkey and Poland launched in the last 18 months
  — The r12 book comes out in December
  — The church-wide campaign is ready to launch in 2010
  — Radio audience grew by 100,000 this year
  — We have an awesome staff and excellent, supportive Board

There is so much to thank You for Lord God almighty. I thank You and praise You for showering Your love and blessing on my life.

I long to walk in a manner worthy of my calling. Give Your strength and wisdom today Lord to tackle what will come my way today. Amen!

That did a lot for me. It changed my Saturday. I couldn't wait to get to work. My circumstances didn't change. There was still rubble, but there was God. There was still a gray zone, but it was shrinking under the glare of God's glory. That's what God wants us to do—battle discouragement with His help.

### Fight! Fight! Fight!

Do you want me to home in on that point some more? Again I say, "Fight!" When you are discouraged, you have to reach down and fight. When you feel like fighting, fight. When you don't feel like fighting, fight. Holy ambition takes root in us the more we realize the stakes involved in living in this world where God has decided He will actually accomplish great things through frail, weak, and prone-to-discouragement people like us. Holy ambition includes the six conditions we have examined in these pages. They make a great battle plan. They even include a strategy about what to do when the war doesn't seem to be going our way. We must refuse to give up when we suffer the reverses of discouragement. We must keep fighting.

Nehemiah positioned the people on the wall and he said, "Look, there is so much to lose we can't afford not to fight. Think of your wives, sons, and daughters and your future. What about God's reputation? Remember the Lord and fight!"

There is so much to lose when we get discouraged, and the only way we can keep from giving up is to keep fighting. When the apostle Paul looked back over his years of serving Christ, he used battle language to describe his life and ministry: "I have fought the good fight, I have finished the race, I have kept the faith" (2 Timothy 4:7). Faith is not a feeling. The way faith is restored involves taking one step in the right direction. Even, or especially, when you don't feel like it. Sometimes taking a step in the right direction hurts, but we must do it anyway. That's how we fight the fight, run our race, and keep the faith. Nehemiah did that; so did Paul. And so can you!

### Never Fight Alone

Nehemiah first organized the work so that everyone could make a contribution to the whole. When discouragement came, he regrouped the people in families so that they would have some positive relationships. But the work still had to be done; the fight had to go on. So Nehemiah added the back-up feature. "When discouragement or attack of any kind comes," he told the people, "call for back-up and we'll be there! We're going to be in this together."

The last few verses in chapter 4 provide a picture of a motivated daily routine.

So we continued the work with half the men holding spears, from the first light of dawn till the stars came out. At that time I also said to the people, "Have every man and his helper stay inside Jerusalem at night, so they can serve us as guards by night and workmen by day." Neither I nor my brothers nor my men nor the guards with me took off our clothes; each had his weapon, even when he went for water.

NEHEMIAH 4:21–23

Sometimes the work takes all day. A great task for God can involve concentrated periods of total effort. That kind of commitment takes a toll almost immediately if we try to work alone. One of the features that will leap out at you as you review all the conditions and elements of holy ambition is the number of times others need to be involved. Holy ambition will express God's work in your life using many other people. Never fight alone.

Nehemiah led a group to accomplish what seemed impossible because he kept them together. He helped them develop courageous souls. And God demonstrated in that amazing achievement just how strongly He supports those whose hearts are completely His.

## THE STRATEGY FOR A COURAGEOUS SOUL

Because this chapter is crucial to your survival as you seek to develop holy ambition, I want to end with a strategic outline to which you can refer in the inevitable times of difficulty that will come. Use it as a quick guide to tough times. As I mentioned at the outset, I deeply desire to prepare you for what is ahead. I can see in Nehemiah's life and I've learned in my own life, that when I prepare for the tough times, I respond more often in a way that pleases God.

So when you feel like the way of holy ambition is too difficult, remember that you were told to expect that. When you want to give up, consider yourself on familiar ground. When you feel overwhelmed, take heart. You are not alone. Use the following sketch of the obstacles to holy ambition and the responses of a courageous soul. Retrace your steps and resume your journey toward making a difference for God.

Three *clues* to the presence of opposition:

    § Ridicule

    § Criticism

    § Discouragement

Four *causes* of discouragement:

    § Loss of strength — you're tired.

- Loss of vision and perspective—you're feeling confused.

- Loss of confidence—you're feeling uncertain.

- Loss of security—you're feeling vulnerable.


Four keys to overcome discouragement and maintain a courageous soul:

- Be proactive: Do something practical and positive.

- Remember who's on your team: Remember the Lord.

- Fight! Fight! Fight!

- Never fight alone.

**Question from Chip on the video:** *Where do you feel most overwhelmed and where do you feel most discouraged?*

**1.** As we have seen from Nehemiah, pursuing your holy ambition doesn't mean a life of smooth spiritual sailing (page 155). As you think about pursuing your holy ambition where can you expect difficulty and even opposition?

**2.** Read Nehemiah 4:1–2. No sooner had Nehemiah started rebuilding the wall and he became the target of ridicule and criticism. Someone has said "Compliments are written in sand and criticism is written in wet cement." For some of us, criticism has deep and lasting impact. Share honestly how you deal with criticism and the impact it has on you.

**3.** In this chapter, Chip talks about "flying your flag"—going public with your faith (page 160). Has there been a time when you took a stand for your faith? What were the results and how did you grow from it?

**4.** Do you sense that there is an area or situation in your life right now where God is asking you to be more courageous?

**5.** Chip said that loss of strength (fatigue) is one of the causes of discouragement in our lives. When you get fatigued, what are some of the indicators? What would your family say are the signs of fatigue in your life?

**6.** Read Nehemiah 4:10–12. They are right in the middle of a massive project and discouragement sets in. How much do you struggle with discouragement? When are you most susceptible to discouragement?

**7.** Nehemiah had been a faithful servant and like the apostle Paul, could say, "I have fought the good fight, I have finished the race, I have kept the faith" (2 Timothy 4:7). As you think about getting to the end of your life, what are 3 statements you would like to be said of you that would show you had been a faithful servant?

**From Chip on the video:** After your discussion time, break up into groups of three and spend the last few minutes praying with and for one another.

## LIVE IT OUT

1. Set aside some time this week to do a serious study of Nehemiah 4-6. Then, review Chip's outline on p. 178–79. Which one of these key ideas do you most need to be aware of or put into practice?

2. Just do it. If God has placed on your heart a holy ambition, don't let it die with the completion of this study. Decide what is your next step to keep moving forward and DO IT.

# holy
# AMBITION
where do we go from here?

---

Two men, separated by almost five hundred years, arrived at Jerusalem. For each, the city was the destination of a long journey with a great purpose. They may have even walked the same road, approaching the Holy City from the east. Each had, from a certain point on the road, a panoramic view of the entire city from a distance, covering a mountaintop.

One, Nehemiah, was coming to the end of a long trip from Persia. His first sight of the city must have created a jumble of emotions: relief in a journey's end, excitement over another unfolding chapter in God's guidance, and joy in seeing the great city and the temple, shining in the sun.

But there must have also been a rising tide of grief over the extent of the devastation that lay before him. No doubt Nehemiah stopped in his tracks. The images created by his brother's report that had dislocated Nehemiah's heart months ago were shattered by the stark reality of the ruins and wreckage across the valley. Piled rocks and gaping holes marked the previous existence of walls. Charred remains announced the fate of gates that had once guarded the city. A new and shocking realization of the task ahead must have struck Nehemiah with the force of a punch.

We don't know how Nehemiah reacted immediately to the sight of the city, but we do know that his purpose was not derailed. We know that whatever the feelings or thoughts about the task that flooded his heart and mind when he actually saw the city for the first time, Nehemiah stayed the course. A week later he had galvanized the population into a task that would create a notch on the timeline of history. He lived and acted by holy ambition. Others followed. Nehemiah made a difference for God.

Centuries later another man approached the same city. The day was just starting as Jesus walked toward Jerusalem. He was surrounded by cheering crowds; honored by shouts, by coats dropped, and by palm branches waved. The colt on which He rode reminded some that He was entering the City of David as a King. An observer might have considered this a great moment of triumph for Jesus. Some certainly thought He had arrived to challenge the Roman domination of Israel.

With the sun behind Him, Jesus rounded the last corner on the high road between Bethany and Jerusalem. He gazed across the valley at the city, perhaps in the same spot from which Nehemiah had gotten his first glimpse of Jerusalem so long before. We know how Jesus responded in that moment. He wept. Those close enough heard Him say,

> "If you, even you, had only known on this day what would bring you peace
> —but now it is hidden from your eyes. The days will come upon you
> when your enemies will build an embankment against you and encircle you
> and hem you in on every side. They will dash you to the ground, you and the
> children within your walls. They will not leave one stone on another, because
> you did not recognize the time of God's coming to you."

> LUKE 19:42–44

Nehemiah saw the physical condition of the city; Jesus could see its spiritual condition.

Like Nehemiah, the sight of the city and the task before Him did not derail Jesus' holy ambition. A week later, He, too, changed history. A week later, He, too, galvanized a movement that would transform the world. A week later He defeated death, rose from the grave, secured the way of salvation for people, and launched a message that is still known simply as the good news.

Like Nehemiah, Jesus gave us an example of how to live by holy ambition. He had all the conditions. He faced all the challenges. He proved He is our perfect model. God inspired the writer of Hebrews to put it as well as anyone in Scripture: "Let us fix our eyes on Jesus, the author and perfecter of our faith, who for the joy set before him endured the cross, scorning its shame, and sat down at the right hand of the throne of God. Consider him who endured such opposition from sinful men, so that you will not grow weary and lose heart" (Hebrews 12:2–3).

So we come to the end of this book but quite possibly the beginning of a new chapter for you. I trust that you have already implemented many of the lessons we've learned from Nehemiah. Clearly, we have only scratched the surface. *I don't want you to "grow weary and lose heart." I want you to experience the joy of a life that makes a difference for God.* What you have before you is enough to make some important decisions.

Do you want to live a life of holy ambition? Are you determined to discover what God has planned for your life and to invest yourself fully in that? You will accomplish that only to the degree that the six conditions we have examined are true of your life:

1. A dislocated heart
2. A broken spirit
3. A radical faith
4. A strategic plan
5. A personal commitment
6. A courageous soul

One of those conditions represents a starting point for you today, right now. Which of those conditions do you sense is primary on God's agenda for you? Can you circle and date that one on the list above?

Recent events in the world have reminded us again that safety and comfort in this world are fragile. Just as the news from a far place dislocated Nehemiah's heart, so local news has affected many of us deeply. Terrorist attacks and bio-chemical warfare have become a possibility in places we previously considered safe. Our priorities have been shaken. We have had to answer questions and address fears that were once distant and theoretical but have now moved into our homes.

*We have opportunities today as never before to practice what we believe. We can allow circumstances to cow and silence us, or we can see the shaking of the nations as the opening of doors so that people of holy ambition can make a difference for God.* The world has seen the terror and destruction that people of unholy ambition can wreak. It's time again to be available for God to show the world what His people can accomplish. Start by making sure that your heart, your life, belongs to God unconditionally.

"For the eyes of the Lord move to and fro throughout the earth that He may strongly support those whose heart is completely His" (2 Chronicles 16:9 NASB). You can count on God's support as you seek to live by holy ambition.

# acknowledgments

Over the years I have developed a habit that has been very profitable for me. I've written out on 3 x 5 cards the dreams or desires I believe God has put on my heart. Some fifteen years ago, I wrote, "I'd like to put some truth and messages into book form in a way that would really serve people in a powerful way." When I wrote those words, the goal seemed not only impossible but semi-ridiculous. But books have been such an instrumental part of my spiritual growth, I dreamed that one day God would allow me to put some truth in printed form to serve people the way others have served me. This book is the first of many He has allowed me to write, and I am forever grateful and indebted to that original group of people who made it possible.

The following list of acknowledgments in no way covers all the bases, but it begins to recognize the many people responsible for this book's coming to completion and, I pray, serving you, the reader, in a powerful and significant way.

- ❧ I have to begin with my wife, Theresa, who is my best friend, strongest supporter, and the most godly person I know. Her patience with me, prayer for this project, and love for me through thick and thin is beyond what any man could ask for.

- ❧ Along with Theresa, those who have provided the most encouragement have been the four I have the privilege of calling my children. Eric, Jason, Ryan, and Annie have prayed, encouraged, and asked the kind of questions that have helped shape my life and this book. In each of their lives I see holy ambition being lived out in the place God has them. I am so grateful that God gave me these kids who have been with me on my journey of holy ambition and are a major part of shaping my life.

- ❧ I want to thank the "Prime Movers" for helping me see what God can do through people of influence and affluence when their hearts beat with a holy ambition.

§ I want to thank the elders, staff, and the people of Santa Cruz Bible Church for listening to these truths when first taught and giving me honest feedback all along the way.

§ A special word of thanks goes to Annette Kypreos, my personal assistant. Her tireless work and organizational skill have brought this project from a dream to a reality. Her coordination and administrative savvy have been a delight to me, my partner in this project, Neil Wilson, and the people of Moody Publishers.

§ Speaking of people who turn dreams into reality, I've got to thank Neil Wilson, my editor and fellow wordsmith in the project. Neil's heart for God and his ministry mind-set along with the ability to help me take that which was spoken and place it into written form was priceless. What a joy to work with him and see spiritual synergy right before our eyes.

§ I also want to thank Greg Thornton and the entire team at Moody Publishers. If it weren't for them, this book would never have become a reality. It was over lunch in downtown Chicago that God used them to convince me that the first book must be one that communicates my life message. Their cooperation and flexibility have been beyond anything anyone could ask.

§ The support of Moody Bible Institute and the excellent expertise of the Living on the Edge staff and executive team have allowed us to put this truth in a small group DVD format to help groups around the world.

§ A special thanks to Lance Witt for his work on the small group section of this book. He is a mentor, friend, and man with a holy ambition to help pastors.

§ And, finally, the man who wrote the foreword to this book is the one who introduced me to Nehemiah and launched me on a journey of inductive Bible study that has shaped my life and ministry. "Prof" Hendricks has been my mentor, friend, and hero for almost two decades. I'm one of your 2 Timothy 2:2 men, Prof. Thank you!

# How did *Holy Ambition* impact you?

## Who else needs to learn how to turn their God-shaped dreams into a reality?

Launch a Small
Group *Today*.

# THE MIRACLE OF LIFE CHANGE

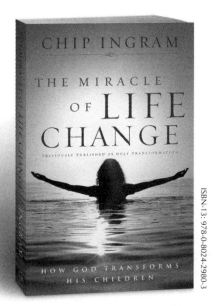

ISBN-13: 978-0-8024-2980-3

So, you've been "born again"...now what? You were made for intimacy, beauty, impact, and adventure, but you still struggle to break old habits and keep your temper in check. Is it really possible to become more like Christ? It is! In this series, Chip explores how life-change really happens, even in the midst of frustrating, painful, or mundane circumstances. Don't give up!

www.MoodyPublishers.com

# CHARACTER COUNTS

ISBN-13: 978-0-8024-3909-3

Character and conduct are inextricably connected. Today's headlines highlight society's problems, but then the pundits simplistically push the blame off on big business, big government, or some other faceless entity. Yet—with the exception of natural disasters—most problems are caused by people . . . people who put money, power, or personal gain ahead of the bedrock values of character and integrity. We are all now collectively paying the price for years of selfish excess brought on by these behaviors.

MOODY
PUBLISHERS
www.MoodyPublishers.com

# A Life that Matters

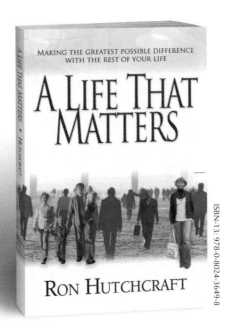

ISBN-13: 978-0-8024-3649-8

Greatness—lasting greatness—is a desire built into every human heart. For the believer in Christ, it is not only possible, but expected. How will your life matter? God wants your life to count for eternity. He wants you to join the team of rescuers He is sending into a desperate world.

MOODY
PUBLISHERS

www.MoodyPublishers.com